NATURE MACRAMÉ

20+ STUNNING PROJECTS INSPIRED BY MOUNTAINS, OCEANS, DESERTS, & MORE

Rachel Breuklander

creator of The Lark's Head Shop

PAGE STREET
PUBLISHING CO.

PAGE STREET
PUBLISHING CO.

First published in 2022 by
Page Street Publishing Co.
27 Congress Street, Suite 1511
Salem, MA 01970
www.pagestreetpublishing.com

Distributed by Macmillan, sales in Canada by The Canadian Manda Group.

26   25   24   23   22   1 2   3   4   5

ISBN-13: 978-1-64567-604-1
ISBN-10: 1-64567-605-8

Library of Congress Control Number: 2022933683

Cover and book design by Emma Hardy for Page Street Publishing Co.
Photography by Rachel Breuklander and Sophia Acosta

Printed and bound in The United States of America

TABLE OF CONTENTS

INTRODUCTION

Macramé has made a strong return to the world of home décor in the last few years, and it's here to stay. It's no wonder so many people are dipping their toes into this art form; macramé is easy to pick up, and the process itself has been described by many as meditative and therapeutic. Plus, the possibilities are truly endless when it comes to what you can make. From tiny knotted sculptures to two-story installations, whatever you can dream up, you can create.

For me, macramé has been a way to reconnect with my own creativity and my passion for nature. Whether it's hiking up a mountain, going camping, or taking a solitary day trip to the desert to center myself, I've always found peace and fulfillment in the outdoors. Once I had grown more experienced in the processes of macramé, I began to seek inspiration for my work in nature. Luckily, living in California meant I was never short of material; an hour's drive in any direction would either take me to vast deserts, thick forests, and mountains, or some of the world's most beautiful beaches.

Nature has a way of centering us and bringing our focus back to what really matters in life. Few things can make us feel more alive and present than standing out at the edge of the ocean and feeling the mist spraying our cheeks, or looking out over the top of the mountain at miles and miles of endless, cascading peaks. Nature moves us and heals us in more ways than one.

Needless to say, macramé and nature are truly a perfect combination. There are so many ways to experience the connection with nature in macramé, whether it is creating nature-inspired pieces, incorporating earthy materials and fibers into your work, or simply by soaking in the warm sunshine and fresh air as you knot in your backyard.

In this book, you will learn all of the skills needed to start your journey with macramé (or find new creative inspiration if you have already been tying knots for some time). Each project has a loose nature theme, from abstract desert landscapes to useful pouches for mushroom foraging. The projects are divided into chapters based on four themes: desert, mountain and forest, ocean, and earth and sky. Within each chapter, the projects are arranged by difficulty from beginner to advanced. It is my hope that working through these projects will inspire you to bring a bit more nature into your life as well as your home.

WHAT YOU'LL NEED

Macramé is a very simple craft in that the main tools used to create the knots are your own hands. It doesn't take a lot to get started, but there are several different types of cording out there to choose from, and plenty of accessories and tools that can take your pieces to the next level or make the work itself a bit easier. In this section, I outline the different types of fiber and their characteristics, some workstation equipment and tools, and some additional accessories and tools that will help in the process of creating.

the essentials

fiber

While macramé can be created using virtually any type of fiber, we will be using various types of cotton cord throughout the entirety of this book. Rope, string, and braided cord are all examples of specific types of cord. Each project materials list will specify the recommended type and size (in diameter) of cord. The diameter is the most important thing to keep consistent with the pattern. The projects can sometimes still work with a different type or color of cord than what is recommended, but keep in mind that the outcome of the project will look different.

Here are the three main types of cotton cord and their differences:

- Rope: Typically consists of three cotton strands twisted together (3-ply). Macramé rope is sturdy and structured, making it great for projects that need to be strong or have a more geometric, structured look. This type of cord is easy to tie and untie, and it will not lose its integrity, making it great for beginners or very precise, structured pieces.

- String: Consists of one strand of multiple fibers twisted together. It is much softer on the hands than rope and doesn't cause blisters even when working with it for a long time. It also combs out into a beautiful smooth fringe. It does unravel or untwist more easily than rope, especially if it undergoes a lot of friction from unknotting or even by dragging against other strings too much while knotting. This type of cord works great for wall hangings and pieces that feature fringe or tassels.

- Braided cord: Consists of several thinner strands of string that are woven together instead of twisted. Braided cord tends to be the sturdiest, but it is very difficult to comb into fringe. Like rope, braided cord is best used for projects needing extra structure or strength.

For suggestions on where to source quality fibers, check out page 24.

anchors

Anchors refer to the main object to which the macramé project will be attached. Some examples of anchors include:

- Dowels (for wall hangings): branches, wooden dowels, or metal dowels
- Wood/metal rings and hoops (for plant hangers or circular wall hangings)
- Keychain clasps
- Earring hardware or frames

The materials list for each project will specify the recommended anchor to be used for that specific project. It is usually acceptable to substitute one type of dowel for another based on personal preference. When selecting a dowel, a diameter of around 1 to 2 inches (2.5 to 5 cm) is usually a good size for most projects, but larger projects may benefit from a thicker diameter because the piece will be heavier. If using branches, I recommend trying to find a relatively straight and smooth branch. Test the branch out before starting, making sure that it doesn't snap easily.

Branches or driftwood can either be found locally (I find all of mine on hikes and in wooded areas near me) or sourced online. Wood or metal dowels can be purchased at home improvement stores. Rings and hoops of various sizes, as well as keychain and earring hardware, can usually be bought at your local craft store or online.

fabric scissors

A sharp pair of shears is a staple tool for any macramé creator. While all-purpose scissors might get you by for your first few projects, they often become too dull and just bend string instead of cutting it cleanly. A good pair of scissors, specifically meant for cutting fabric, will make life much easier and leave your work with crisp and clean cuts. A variety of fabric scissors can be found at virtually any craft store.

fabric measuring tape

Another item that should be readily available in most craft stores, fabric measuring tape is essential for cutting cord to precise measurements. Measuring cord prior to cutting can help reduce waste by preventing overcutting or overestimating cord lengths.

workstation equipment

working rack

A macramé working rack is simply a garment rack repurposed to hold projects as you work or to store completed projects. Garment racks can be found at most general merchandise retailers. Ikea, for example, has some great affordable options.

s-hooks

S-hooks are exactly what they sound like—hooks that are shaped like an "S." The top hook hangs over the working rack, while the bottom hook holds up the anchor for the project. I recommend searching for larger S-hooks (over 4 inches [10 cm] in length, if possible) so that the hooks will be large enough to hold even a thicker branch or dowel. S-hooks can be stacked on each other to lower a project, which can be helpful in adjusting the height of the project to a comfortable point for working.

clipboard

Clipboards are used to secure a project at a specific point so that it stays put while working. These can be found at any office supply retailer. Alternatively, you can use a foam project board with T-pins to pin the project down or simply tape the project to a flat work surface.

other tools and accessories

comb

Any standard comb should work for brushing strings out into fringe. Alternatively, a clean pet brush with metal bristles can be used. This will reduce combing time and make it much easier to brush out.

tapestry needle

Tapestry needles are used to weave loose strings in through the back of a project under a previously knotted section. This is how the loose ends are secured before being trimmed off, ensuring that they will not come undone. Also known as yarn needles, tapestry needles come in a variety of sizes and styles. For the projects in this book, I recommend searching for a plastic, large-eye tapestry needle. The ends will be dull, not sharp, and may have a slight crook or bend.

beads

Because macramé cord is thicker than the yarn or twine that most beads are made to fit around, larger beads with a wide-mouth opening are needed. Most craft stores do sell these now, but they can also be found online—just be sure to check the measurement of the opening and compare it to the diameter of the string you'll be using.

LEARNING THE KNOTS

This section is where you will find detailed step-by-step photos and instructions on all of the classic macramé knots, as well as some lesser known knots and knot variations that will come in handy for some specific designs. I'll also show you all of the secrets behind my signature knotting technique, the alternating colors square knot method (page 21), which we will use for several patterns throughout this book.

classic lark's head knot

This is one of the most common macramé knots, used to attach cord to another item such as a dowel or branch.

 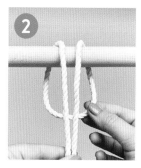 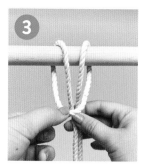 

Step 1: Fold the string in half and hold it at the center point, forming a loop.

Step 2: Toss the loop over the item you'd like to attach it to, from front to back.

Step 3: Thread the loose ends of the cord in front through the loop in the back.

Step 4: Pull the loose ends to tighten the knot.

reverse lark's head knot

The same knot as the classic lark's head, but working in the opposite direction. This knot is simply used as an alternative to the classic lark's head knot for aesthetic purposes.

   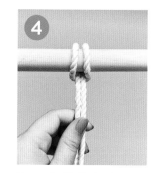

Step 1: Fold the string in half and hold it at the center point, forming a loop. Place the loop behind the item you're attaching the cord to.

Step 2: Toss the loop over the top of the item, from back to front.

Step 3: Thread the loose ends of the cord through the loop in the front.

Step 4: Pull the loose ends to tighten the knot.

single strand lark's head knot

This is another way of tying a lark's head knot when you only have one side of the cord or one lead strand to work with.

Step 1: Toss one side of the string over the top of the item you're attaching it to, going from front to back.

Step 2: Pick up the loose end of the string in the back and cross it over the front cord and then to the right.

Step 3: Move the same loose end behind the dowel and up.

Step 4: Toss the string over the top of the dowel, from back to front.

Step 5: Feed the loose end through the loop you've created in the front.

Step 6: Pull the loose ends to tighten the knot.

constrictor knot

This knot is yet another method used to securely attach a string to an object. In macramé, this is commonly used to attach the "hanger strings" to a wall hanging.

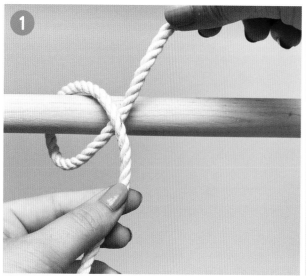

Step 1: Start toward the end of one piece of cord. Loop the shorter end around the dowel by feeding it behind the bottom of the dowel and then back across the top and to the right.

Step 2: Move the shorter end behind the bottom of the dowel again and cross it back over the top.

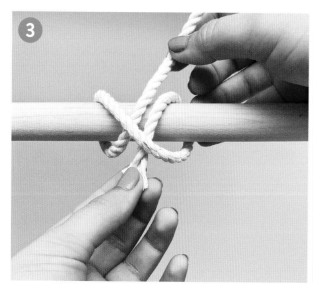

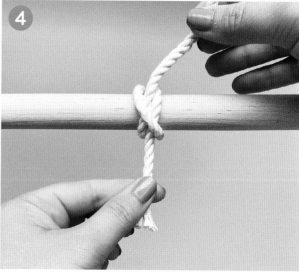

Step 3: Feed the end through the diagonal loop created in the last step.

Step 4: Pull both ends of the cord to tighten or adjust. Trim off the shorter end if needed.

square knot

Probably the most common knot, the square knot is used to tie rope around an object or create designs and texture. This knot typically utilizes four cords, but more can be used either as lead cords or working cords, if desired.

Step 1: Start with four cords. The outer two strings will be doing all of the work, and the inner two strings will stay put.

Step 2: Take the left string and create a loose "4" shape over the other strings, crossing over the two center strings and under the last string.

Step 3: Now, take the right string that is not forming the "4" and cross it to the left, over the left string and behind the two center strings.

Step 4: Bring the string from step 3 forward through the loop that was created in step 2 when making the "4" shape. Pull both outer strings to tighten the knot and adjust its position.

Step 5: Use the right string to create a backward "4" shape. Cross it over the two center strings and under the leftmost string.

Step 6: Take the left string that is not forming the backward "4" and cross it to the right, over the right string and behind the two center strands.

Step 7: Bring that string forward through the loop created when making the backward "4" shape.

Step 8: Now pull the outer strings to tighten and complete the knot.

square knot picot

This square knot variation is used to create loops on the sides of each square knot. It is used to add texture and variety to a design.

Step 1: Start by tying one square knot at the desired starting point.

Step 2: Leaving a space underneath the first square knot, tie another square knot directly beneath.

Step 3: Place your thumb beneath the lower square knot while holding the two center cords firmly in place.

Step 4: Push upward with your thumb to slide the lower square knot up toward the top square knot.

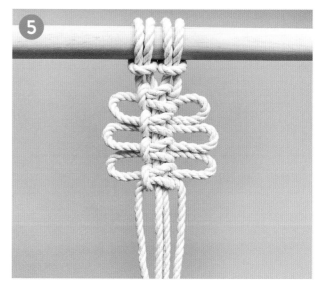

Step 5: Repeat the process as many times as needed; for larger loops, space the square knots farther apart and for smaller loops, space them closer together.

diagonal clove hitch knot

Also known as the diagonal double half-hitch knot, this is the knot used to form a raised diagonal line.

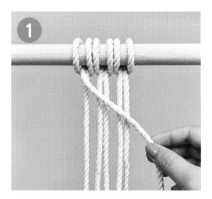

Step 1: Determine the lead cord, meaning the cord that will form the direction of the line you're creating. This lead rope will stay put, while all other strings will be knotted around it. Cross the lead string over the other strings in the desired direction and angle.

Step 2: Pick up the next string over from the lead cord and form a loop around the lead cord, pulling the working cord around and up.

Step 3: Pull the working cord tight.

Step 4: Use the same working cord and loop it around the lead cord just as you did in step 2, pulling the working cord around and up.

Step 5: Gently pull the working cord tight until the knot is secure.

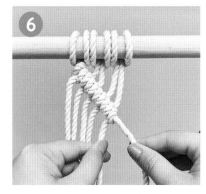

Step 6: Repeat steps 2 to 5 with all of the remaining strings to form a diagonal line.

horizontal clove hitch knot

Also known as the horizontal double half-hitch knot, this is the knot used to form a raised horizontal line.

Step 1: Determine the lead cord, meaning the cord that will form the direction of the line you're creating. This lead string will stay put, while all other strings will be knotted around it. Hold the lead string over the other strings at a horizontal angle.

Step 2: Pick up the next string over from the lead cord and form a loop around the lead cord, pulling the working cord down and toward the outer edge.

Step 3: Pull the working cord tight.

Step 4: Use the same working cord and loop it around the lead cord just as you did in step 2, pulling the working cord down and between the two loops created.

Step 5: Gently pull the working cord tight until the knot is secure.

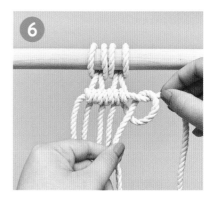

Step 6: Repeat steps 2 to 5 with all of the remaining working strings to form a horizontal line.

vertical clove hitch knot

Also known as the vertical double half-hitch knot, this knot forms a raised vertical line. In this variation of the clove hitch knots, all of the hanging strings are the lead cords and a working cord is typically an extra cord that is introduced in. Often, a section of two hanging cords will be grouped together as one lead cord "bundle," meaning that the working cord is tied around two strings at a time.

Step 1: Take the working cord and place it behind the first lead cord (or pair of lead cords as demonstrated here). The majority of the length of the working cord should be toward the inside, with only a few inches of length on the outer edge.

Step 2: Loop the longer end of the working cord around the lead cords, ending with the cord at the top.

Step 3: Pull the working cord from both sides to tighten.

Step 4: Use the working cord to loop it around the lead cords just as you did in steps 2 and 3, pulling the working cord to the same side and feeding it through the loop.

Step 5: Gently pull the working cord tight until the knot is secure.

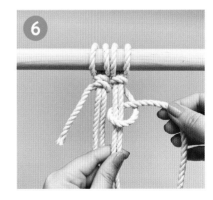

Step 6: Use the same working cord to move to the next lead cord(s) on the right, using the same technique to create horizontal rows of vertical clove hitch knots.

gathering knot

This knot is used to secure a bundle of cords together. It is often used in plant hangers, keychains, or tassels.

Step 1: Use a separate cord from the cords you are trying to bundle. Form a small loop at one end, with the longer side of the string on the right.

Step 2: Place the loop against the back of a bundle of cords, then cross the longer end of the string over to the left side.

Step 3: Bring that end of the string behind the bundle and begin to wrap it around.

Step 4: Wrap the string around as needed, moving from top to bottom and making sure to leave the bottom of the loop exposed.

Step 5: Once the bundle has been wrapped enough times, take the loose end of the string and thread it through the bottom loop.

Step 6: Now, take the loose string from the top and gently pull it upward. This will tighten the loop at the bottom and hide it underneath the wrapped section, securing the knot.

Step 7: Once the knot is tightened and the loop is hidden, trim the loose end from the top and the bottom as close to the gathering knot as possible.

rya knot

In macramé, this knot is often used to add fringe or tassels to an area in the design. It can also be used to add color.

Step 1: Place the center of a loose string horizontally at the place in the design where you would like to attach it. Pick two strings to attach it to; in this case, the two center white strings.

Step 2: Push both ends of the loose string through to the back of the two center strings.

Step 3: Take the left side of the loose string and feed it back through to the front, between the two white strings.

Step 4: Take the right side of the loose string and feed it back through to the front in the center as well.

Step 5: Pull both loose ends to form a tight knot.

adding color

alternating colors square knot method

This is a technique I developed in order to create my original landscape designs. It relies on switching colors of string and tying alternating square knots to create a unique, beautiful pattern!

attaching the first color

Step 1: Begin by placing the center of the colored cord horizontally behind four hanging strings.

Step 2: Cross the left side over the center strings and to the right, placing it under the right cord.

Step 3: Take the right side of the colored cord and feed it behind the center strings, and forward through the loop on the left.

Step 4: Pull to tighten the knot and slide up to the top of the strings.

Step 5: Continue as you would a regular square knot: Create a backward "4" shape and feed the outer string behind the center strings and through the loop on the right.

Step 6: Tie continuous square knots.

switching colors

Step 1: Place the center of the new string color behind all of the other strings.

Step 2: Push the old colored string toward the back while keeping the center strings forward.

Step 3: Cross the left side of the new color over the center strings and to the right, placing it under the right side of the cord.

Step 4: Take the right side of the new colored cord and feed it behind the center strings and back to the front through the loop on the left.

Step 5: Pull to tighten the knot and slide it up so that this knot is directly under the last knot of the previous color.

Step 6: Continue as you would a regular square knot: Create a backward "4" shape and feed the outer string behind the center strings and through the loop on the right.

Step 7: If you will no longer be needing the strings from the previous color, move them to the back and trim off the loose ends of the previous section after tying one full square knot. If you will be switching back to the previous color at a later step, continue knotting over the previous colored cords and then see "Switching Back to a Previous Color."

switching back to a previous color

Step 1: Bring the ends of the previous color back to the front, while pushing the most recent working strings to the back.

Step 2: Use the previous colored strings to tie a new square knot over all the strings, making sure the last section's strings are in the back.

Step 3: Continue tying square knots, trimming off the last section in the back, if needed.

TIPS AND TRICKS

After building up my own experience with this craft, I have learned that there are tons of tips and tricks that could have saved me a lot of time (and a couple of headaches) in the beginning of my journey, if I had only known! That's why I'm so happy to share some of my best tips and practices with you, to make this craft as fun and enjoyable as possible.

practice the knots

When learning macramé, there are only a few knots that are absolutely essential to getting started. The three most commonly used knots are the square knot (page 13), the lark's head knot (page 10), and the clove hitch knot (aka the double half-hitch knot [page 16]). Before starting your first project, it may be helpful to practice and build some muscle memory with the different knots. I recommend using some lower cost twine, cord, or yarn that will hold its shape well before working with a higher quality or more expensive string.

undoing knots

The great thing about macramé is that it is very forgiving of mistakes—it's not like painting where once something is on the canvas, it is permanent. If you make a mistake, it is absolutely okay to untie the knot and try again! When untying knots, be as gentle as possible while pulling them apart so as to preserve the integrity of the cord. If you notice the bottoms of the cord unraveling, it may be helpful to either tie an overhand knot right above the ends or wrap some tape around them.

tension

Tension is one of the most important things to perfect in macramé. Perfect tension will create a neat, uniform look in a piece. Tying knots too loose can give an unfinished, messy look, while tying knots too tight can cause the strings to distort and even hurt your hands after a while. Learning to maintain the correct tension takes time and practice, but as you work be mindful of how tightly you are pulling the strings and make sure you keep it consistent across the entire piece.

finding quality supplies

Often in macramé, higher quality supplies lead to higher quality pieces. Most macramé tools and accessories can be purchased at craft stores, hardware stores, or through a quick Google search. The search for high-quality fibers can be a little trickier, as many large craft retailers don't sell large quantities of macramé cording. There are smaller suppliers in many countries that source quality macramé materials and cord to provide to the community of makers. Many suppliers can be found through searching on Etsy, Amazon, or social media platforms for macramé supplies—just make sure you are getting 100% cotton fibers for the highest quality and softest feel.

If you'd like to work with the exact cords and colors I used for all of the projects in this book, I supply them through my website at www.thelarksheadshop.com. If you are located in Canada, you can purchase supplies from Lots of Knots Canada via their website www.lotsofknots.ca. If you are located in the UK, you can purchase supplies from Hitch and Arrow via their website www.hitchandarrow.com. And if you are located in Australia, you can purchase supplies from Mary Maker Studio via their website at www.marymakerstudio.com.au.

setting up a workspace

horizontal

Working on a flat surface can be ideal for smaller projects like keychains or jewelry. When working with a horizontal surface, you will usually need some way to anchor down your project. This can be achieved by using a clipboard, some T-pins and a foam mat, or even just by using some tape to hold down the base of the project.

vertical

For larger projects, working on a vertical plane will be much easier. It also prevents unnecessary tangling and knotting of cords as you work. Most macramé artists use a clothing rack and hang the base or anchor of their project on S-hooks. However, there are other alternatives to using a clothing rack as your workstation if you don't have the space or aren't sure about the commitment yet. Some alternatives are:

- Hanging a project on the back of a chair using S-hooks
- Tying a hanger cord to the base of the project and hanging it from a doorknob or a hook on the wall
- Using over-the-door hooks and hanging your project on the back of a door

get comfortable

It can be easy to get so focused on what you're creating that after a while you end up with a stiff neck, sore arms, and achy joints in your hands. Make sure that as you work, you keep your project at a comfortable height where you don't have to reach your arms up too high or crouch down. Take breaks every so often to stretch your back, arms, and hands.

cutting cord

Knowing how much cord to cut for a project can be a daunting task for new macramé enthusiasts. In this book the estimated cord lengths will be provided, and will usually be recommended a bit longer than what is actually needed. However, there are some general rules of thumb that can help when cutting cord.

- Measure twice, cut once. It's easy when cutting large quantities of cord to want to get through it quickly, but there's nothing worse than cutting a handful of cord and then realizing you measured wrong the first time.

- Always overestimate length. Once you're out of string, you're out. It's always better to have extra string at the end than to run out, because that string can be used for smaller projects.

- For most projects, the string will need to be cut four to eight times the total desired length. This amount increases or decreases based on the density of the knots in that project or section. For example, when cutting string for a very loosely knotted piece or section, I would cut four times what the final length would need to be. For a somewhat densely knotted piece, I would cut six times the total desired length, and for a very densely knotted piece, I would cut eight times the total desired length.

- For landscape pieces, all estimates given in this book for cord lengths are based on the largest section needed in that color. If you'd like to save on cord and have less string scraps left over from each landscape project, you can use my rule of cutting the string to ten times the total length of the color in that column because the knots are stacked so tightly together.

working with rope

Working with 3-ply or braided rope can be easier than single-twist string for beginners when first learning and practicing the knots, because it holds its structure a bit better. However, when working with 3-ply rope, the bottoms tend to untwist as the strings are moved around. A way to prevent this while working is to wrap some tape around the bottom of each string right after cutting.

combing fringe

Here are some tips I use to get perfect fringe for feathers and tassels:

- Start from the bottom up. Combing from the top down can sometimes just tangle string even more. Gently brush though the bottom half first, and slowly work your way up.

- Try using a pet brush (a clean one, of course). The sturdy, metal bristles of a pet brush help brush out fringe more quickly. It's a huge time-saver!

- Wear a face covering, because brushing out a bunch of cotton string can send lots of fuzzy particles into the air. A face covering will prevent you from breathing in any of those fibers.

- If the fringe isn't smooth or straight enough, or you are working with 3-ply rope, which tends to result in wavy fringe, try misting the fringe with water and lying it flat, or use a hair straightener to straighten the fibers out.

- Sometimes fringe can tend to twist back over time, especially if the strings are longer. Touching it up with a comb will be helpful from time to time, but the fringe can also be sprayed lightly with some fabric stiffener or even hairspray after combing to keep it in place for longer.

the final trim

Cutting the final trim of the piece can be another intimidating aspect of macramé for beginners and seasoned artists alike. Here are my best tips for trimming the ends:

- Start longer, then slowly work your way up. I always do one rough trim of the piece a few inches longer than I know I'll want it. Then, I move up little by little until I get to the length I want, starting by cutting the longest point first.

- For a straight trim, measure multiple points along the piece and cut one string along several different spots to the desired length, then cut all remaining pieces using those first cuts as guidelines. Alternatively, you can hang the piece up on a wall and apply a piece of tape across the bottom in a straight line, securing the loose strings to the wall so they can't move around while you trim. Then, cut right below the bottom of the tape.

- For a V-shaped or curved trim, start by finding the center point and cut the center few strings as long as you'd like the piece to be. Next, move to the outermost strings and cut them on each side to the shortest length desired. Then, move to the middle point on each side and cut another few strings midway between the shortest and longest lengths. Use these cuts as guidelines when trimming the V-shape.

save scraps

Scraps can be used for so many things in macramé! The smaller pieces can be used to add fringe to another piece or to create fringe tassels, and the longer pieces can be used to make smaller projects like keychains, jewelry, or even mini wall hangings.

MACRAMÉ TERMS

If you're newer to macramé, you might notice some unique terminology and it can be a little overwhelming at first. Here are some commonly used terms and a brief explanation of what they mean and how they apply to this specific craft.

Adjacent: Next to each other.

Alternating: Tying a knot with one cord or group of cords, then switching to tie the same type of knot with another cord or group of cords.

Anchor: The object that a project will be attached to, functioning as its base. Examples include wooden dowels, branches, keychain clasps, or rings.

Bundle: A group of cords that have been gathered together.

Column: A vertical arrangement of knots.

Fringe: A finishing technique in which the loose strings are untwisted, unraveled, or combed out.

Hitch: A knotting action that is used to attach cords to other cords or objects.

Inverted: A term used to describe something flipped upside down. Example: an inverted "V" shape.

Lead cord (aka traveling cord or filler cord): The cord that remains stationary as knots are tied around it.

Loop: The round or circular shape that is created when two parts of a cord are crossed or folded together.

Ply: The number of strands of string that are twisted together to form a rope. For example, 3-ply rope has three separate strands of string that are twisted together while 6-ply has six strands.

Row: A horizontal arrangement of knots.

Sinnet (also spelled sennit): A chain, or column, of identical knots made one after the other.

Tension: The tightness with which a knot is tied.

Weave: Placing cords so that they pass underneath other cords or knots.

Working cord (aka knotting cord): The cord that is used to actually tie knots, sometimes over other stationary cords known as lead cords.

DESERT

It took me a long time to appreciate the beauty of the desert. On the surface it may seem like a barren, dry wasteland. However, a closer look reveals the still beauty of it all. Amidst the harshness of the environment, life bursts at the seams. The night sky lights up with views of the Milky Way and stars, illuminating your surroundings like nothing you'd experience in a city. Wind and sand dance together and erode slowly, creating incredible formations and dunes.

The projects in this chapter will transport you from the quiet painted hills of Death Valley, California, to the forests of giant saguaro cacti in Arizona and everywhere in between. Most of these projects feature the alternating colors square knot method, where we will "paint with fiber" to create landscapes reflecting different kinds of desert scenes, such as wind-sculpted sand dunes and the lush green valleys that contrast the stunning red rock desert formations of Sedona.

PAINTED HILLS DESERT HOOP

level: beginner

This piece was inspired by a picturesque scenic drive through the Artist's Palette in Death Valley, California. While roaming through the foothills of this barren desert, you may stumble across all sorts of hidden treasures, like the colorful swirls of pastel color in the hills. This piece is an ode to the subtle beauty of the hottest desert in the world.

materials

- 5mm string:
  - Yellow/mustard: 26.3 feet (8 m)
  - 2 to 4 different colors (I used dusty blush, rust, mocha, and oatmeal): 44 feet (13.4 m) total
- 10-inch (25.4-cm) metal hoop
- Measuring tape
- Scissors
- Comb

knots used in this project

- Lark's Head Knot (page 10)
- Diagonal Clove Hitch Knot (page 15)
- Single Strand Lark's Head Knot (page 11)
- Reverse Lark's Head Knot (page 10)
- Horizontal Clove Hitch Knot (page 16)

part 1: the sun

TIP: When creating a rounded shape like this using clove hitch knots, remember that with each clove hitch knot you tie, the lead cord needs to be angled in the direction you want the line to form. Therefore, when you are working on the left half of the sun, you will be directing your lead cord downward away from the metal frame. When you work on the right side, the lead cord will need to point back up toward the top of the frame.

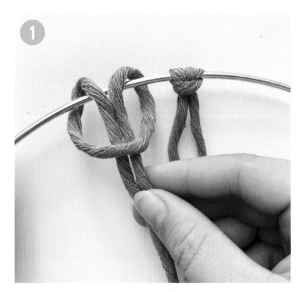

Step 1: Cut seven pieces of yellow string to 45-inch (114.3-cm) lengths. Attach two of the strings to the metal hoop using a standard lark's head knot.

Step 2: Take the second string from the left and cross it over the two strings to the right. This will be the lead cord for the first row of clove hitch knots.

Step 3: Use the two strings to the right to tie diagonal clove hitch knots around the lead cord.

Step 4: Take the lead cord and attach it back to the hoop using a single strand lark's head knot.

Step 5: Attach a new string to the left side using a lark's head knot. The inner hanging string from that lark's head knot will become the new lead cord for the next row of diagonal clove hitch knots. Tie the first two diagonal clove hitch knots, then pause.

Step 6: There will be a bit of a gap between the last working cord and the next one; to fill this gap, attach another yellow string directly to the lead cord using a reverse lark's head knot.

Step 7: Tighten and slide the new string up the lead cord until it sits directly next to the last knot. Resume tying the row of diagonal clove hitch knots and attach the lead cord back to the hoop using a single strand lark's head knot, just like in step 4.

Step 8: Continue adding three more rows of diagonal clove hitch knots using the same method. It shouldn't be necessary to add any additional strings in to fill "gaps" as was done in step 6, but if you notice any gaps you can cut additional strings to add in.

Step 9: Once all rows are complete, trim the loose strings to about 1 inch (2.5 cm) in length.

Step 10: Use the comb to gently brush out the fringe, being cautious not to catch the comb on any of the knots.

Step 11: Complete a final trim on the fringe. Carefully cut a rounded shape, following the curve of the knots.

part 2: the hills

Step 12: Cut the colored strings into 24 pieces total, each measuring 22 inches (56 cm) in length. Starting about 4 inches (10 cm) below the sun, use horizontal clove hitch knots to attach the colored strings to your hoop. Leave 2 inches (5 cm) of string hanging on the outside of the hoop.

Step 13: Attach all 24 strings to the hoop, alternating colors evenly.

Step 14: Once all of the strings are attached, divide them into upper and lower halves and separate the two halves.

Step 15: Cross the lower half on top of the upper half.

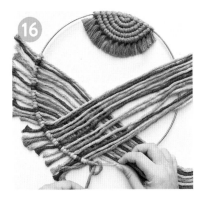

Step 16: Begin attaching the loose string ends back to the other side of the hoop using horizontal clove hitch knots, making sure that none of the strings are tangled or out of order. Continue until all of the strings are secured to the hoop.

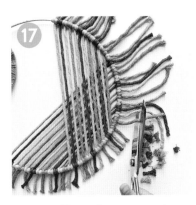

Step 17: Trim all excess string to around 1 inch (2.5 cm) in length.

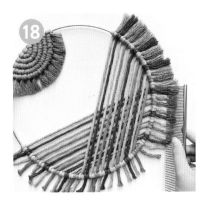

Step 18: Comb out all of the loose strings into fringe.

Step 19: After combing, carefully go through and do a final trim to clean up any uneven ends.

DESERT DUNES LANDSCAPE

level: beginner

There's something truly magical about sand dunes, especially in the last few hours before the sun sets. The light dances along the steep curves of sand, creating such a breathtaking view. This wall hanging is an attempt to capture those little moments of magic in a piece of art.

materials

- 5mm string:
  - White: 165 feet (50.2 m)
  - Yellow/mustard: 13.3 feet (4 m)
  - Rust: 10.5 feet (3.2 m)
  - Dusty blush: 85 feet (25.9 m)
- 14-inch (35.6-cm) branch or dowel
- Measuring tape
- Scissors
- Large tapestry needle
- Comb
- Optional: S-hooks and working rack

knots used in this project

- Reverse Lark's Head Knot (page 10)
- Alternating Colors Square Knot Method (page 21)
- Square Knot (page 13)

Step 1: Cut 24 pieces of white string into 45-inch (114.3-cm) lengths. Attach all 24 pieces to the dowel using a reverse lark's head knot.

Step 2: Cut 12 more pieces of white string into 75-inch (190.5-cm) lengths. Attach each string over a section of four hanging "lead" cords using the alternating colors square knot method. These groups of strings will be referred to as "columns," numbered 1 to 12 (moving from left to right).

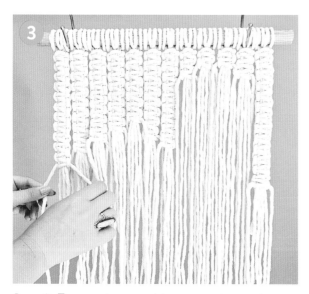

Step 3: Tie continuous white square knots down each column in lengths corresponding to the diagram on page 42.

Step 4: Cut four pieces of yellow string into 40-inch (101.6-cm) lengths. Push the white working cords toward the back, and use the alternating colors square knot method to attach the yellow strings to columns 8 to 11.

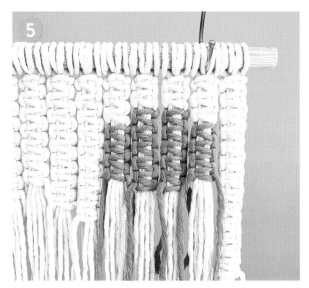

Step 5: Tie continuous yellow square knots down columns 8 to 11 according to the lengths in the diagram. Be sure to tie each yellow square knot over all other strings, including the previous white working strings.

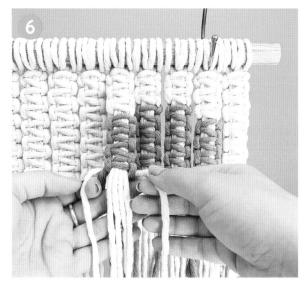

Step 6: After the yellow sections are complete, alternate back to the previous white working cords. Use the white strings to tie a square knot over all other strings in columns 8 to 11.

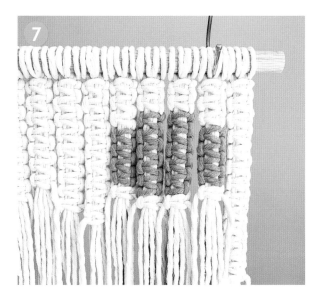

Step 7: After reattaching the white strings in columns 8 to 11 with a square knot, trim the yellow strings off in the back.

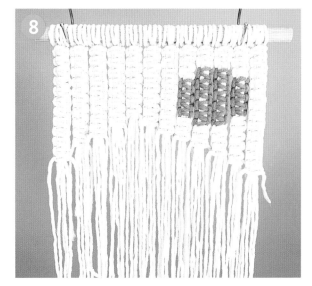

Step 8: Tie continuous white square knots in columns 8 to 11 according to the lengths shown in the diagram.

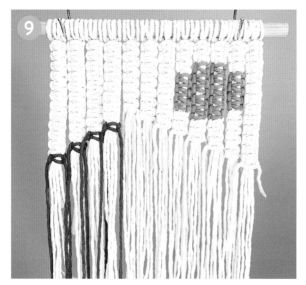

Step 9: Cut five pieces of rust-colored string to 50-inch (127-cm) lengths. Use the alternating colors square knot method to attach rust strings to columns 1 to 4. Save the fifth string for a later step. Trim off the previous white working cords for columns 1 to 4 in the back.

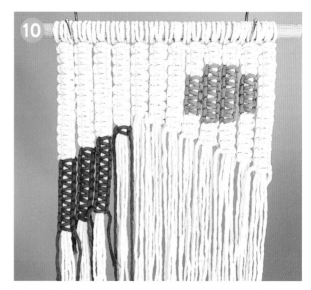

Step 10: Tie continuous rust square knots for columns 1 to 4 according to the lengths in the diagram.

Step 11: Cut three segments of blush string into 40-inch (101.6-cm) lengths. Attach them to columns 1 to 3 using the alternating colors square knot method.

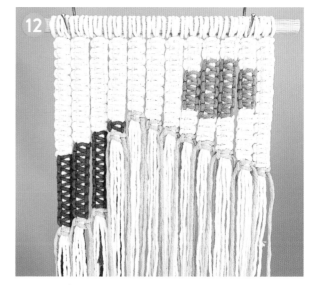

Step 12: Cut nine more blush strings into 100-inch (254-cm) lengths and attach to columns 4 to 12 using the alternating colors square knot method. Once attached, trim the previous working cords off in the back except for column 4.

Step 13: For column 4, tie only two square knots using the blush string and then alternate back to rust by bringing the rust strings forward and pushing the blush strings to the back.

Step 14 (column 4, cont.): Tie 2.5 inches (6.4 cm) of rust square knots before alternating back to the blush string again.

Step 15: For column 5, tie 2 inches (5 cm) of blush square knots, and then attach the last rust string using the alternating colors square knot method.

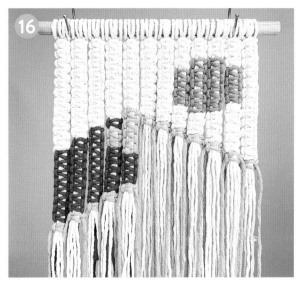

Step 16 (column 5, cont.): Tie 1.5 inches (3.8 cm) of rust square knots, then switch back to blush. Trim off any remaining rust strings for columns 1 to 5 in the back.

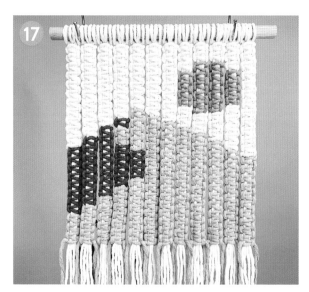

Step 17: Tie blush square knots down each column according to the diagram, forming a straight line across the bottom. If there are any uneven ends, adjust by adding or removing knots as needed. Flip the piece over to the back.

Step 18: Thread each loose working cord through the tapestry needle and weave upward underneath the last square knot to secure. Repeat with each column and then trim any loose ends.

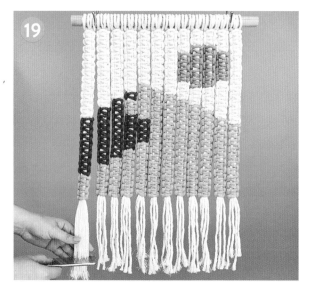

Step 19: Flip the piece back over to the front and use a comb to gently brush out the fringe from the bottom up. Once all the fringe is combed out, trim it to the desired length.

1	2	3	4	5	6	7	8	9	10	11	12
							1.5" (3.8 cm)	1" (2.5 cm)	1" (2.5 cm)	1.5" (3.8 cm)	
							2" (5 cm)	3" (7.6 cm)	3" (7.6 cm)	2" (5 cm)	
			3.5" (8.9 cm)	3.5" (8.9 cm)	4" (10.2 cm)	4.5" (11.4 cm)	1.5" (3.8 cm)	1.5" (3.8 cm)			
5" (12.7 cm)		4" (10.2 cm)	0.5" (1.3 cm)					1.5" (3.8 cm)	1.5" (3.8 cm)		
	4.5" (11.4 cm)		1" (2.5 cm)	2" (5 cm)					2" (5 cm)	3" (7.6 cm)	
			2.5" (6.4 cm)	1.5" (3.8 cm)							7" (17.8 cm)
4" (10.2 cm)	4" (10.2 cm)	4" (10.2 cm)	4" (10.2 cm)								
3" (7.6 cm)	3.5" (8.9 cm)	4" (10.2 cm)	4.5" (11.4 cm)	5" (12.7 cm)	8" (20.3 cm)	7.5" (19 cm)	7" (17.8 cm)	6.5" (16.5 cm)	6" (15.2 cm)	5.5" (14 cm)	5" (12.7 cm)

SAGUARO SUN LANDSCAPE

level: beginner/intermediate

This landscape style piece is inspired by the majestic saguaro cacti in Arizona. Saguaros are massive, often towering over 40 feet (12 m) tall and living up to two hundred years. The Sonoran Desert is the only place in the world to find these cacti, making them extremely rare and special.

This pattern may be a bit more of a challenge due to the more frequent color alternations. I suggest taking a step back between adding new colors to see if you need to add or remove any knots. Ideally, the design will look mostly smooth and not too chunky or pixelated.

materials

- 5mm string:
  - White: 175 feet (53.3 m)
  - Yellow/mustard: 25 feet (7.6 m)
  - Mocha: 70 feet (21.3 m)
  - Oatmeal: 33.3 feet (10.1 m)
- 13-inch (33-cm) branch or dowel
- Measuring tape
- Scissors
- Large tapestry needle
- Comb
- Optional: S-hooks and working rack

knots used in this project

- Reverse Lark's Head Knot (page 10)
- Alternating Colors Square Knot Method (page 21)
- Square Knot (page 13)

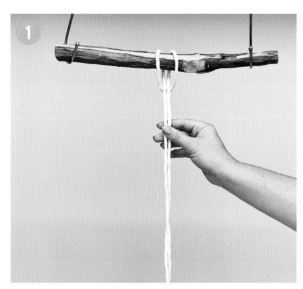

Step 1: Cut 20 pieces of white string into 45-inch (114.3-cm) lengths. Attach all 20 pieces to the branch or dowel by using a reverse lark's head knot.

Step 2: Cut 10 additional pieces of white string to 120-inch (304.8-cm) lengths. Attach each white string over a section of four hanging cords using the alternating colors square knot method. These groups of strings will be referred to as "columns," numbered 1 to 10 (moving from left to right).

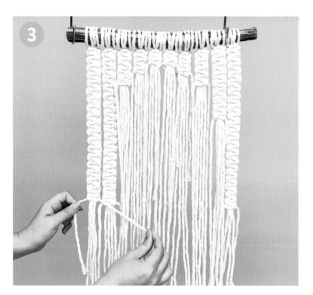

Step 3: After all 10 white strings are attached to the hanging cords, tie continuous square knots down each column according to the measurements outlined in the diagram on page 48.

Step 4: Cut six pieces of yellow string into 50-inch (127-cm) lengths. These will be used for the sun section. In columns 3 to 8, use the alternating colors square knot method to attach the yellow string over all previous strings.

Step 5: You may now trim off the previous white working cords in the back for columns 5, 6, and 7. Do not trim off the white strings for the other columns, as those will be used again. Be very careful not to trim any of the white hanging strings, only the two previous working cords.

Step 6: Tie continuous columns of yellow square knots according to the lengths in the diagram. For columns 3, 4, and 8, continue tying the yellow cords over all six white strings, including the previous white working cords.

Step 7: Once all of the yellow sections are complete, take the white working cords that are in the back of columns 3, 4, and 8, and alternate them back toward the front, pushing the yellow strings to the back.

Step 8: Trim off the yellow strings in the back for columns 3, 4, and 8. Tie continuous white square knots to the lengths corresponding to the diagram for these columns.

Step 9: Cut seven pieces of mocha-colored string for the cactus into 120-inch (304.8-cm) lengths. Attach the mocha string to columns 3 to 9 using the alternating colors square knot method. Trim the previous working cords from the backs of columns 5, 6, and 7 but leave the working cords in the back of columns 3, 4, 8, and 9 to alternate back at a later step.

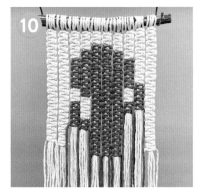

Step 10: Tie continuous square knots to create the cactus shape in columns 3 to 9 in the lengths according to the diagram.

Step 11: Bring the previous white working cords back to the front for sections 3, 4, 8, and 9 while pushing the mocha strings toward the back. Tie square knots in these four columns using the white working cords, then trim off the mocha strings in the back.

Step 12: Complete the columns of white square knots in sections 3, 4, 8, and 9 according to the diagram.

Step 13: Cut 10 pieces of oatmeal-colored string to 40-inch (101.6-cm) lengths for the ground section. Use the alternating colors square knot method to attach the new color to each column. Then, trim the ends off of all previous working cords in the back.

Step 14: Tie continuous square knots in each column according to the lengths in the diagram. The ends should form a straight line across the bottom; if any columns look uneven, you can adjust by adding or removing knots.

Step 15: Flip the piece over to the back. Feed the loose ends of the bottom working cords through the eye of the tapestry needle.

Step 16: Use the needle to weave the strings upward, underneath the last square knot, and pull the string all the way through. Repeat until all working cords are neatly tucked in, then trim the loose ends off.

Step 17: Comb out all hanging strings into fringe and trim the ends to the desired length and style.

1	2	3	4	5	6	7	8	9	10
11" (28 cm)	11.5" (29.2 cm)	2.5" (6.4 cm) 3" (7.6 cm) 1" (2.5 cm) 3" (7.6 cm) 2" (5 cm)	1.5" (3.8 cm) 5" (12.7 cm) 2" (5 cm) 1" (2.5 cm) 1.5" (3.8 cm)	1" (2.5 cm) 2.5" (6.4 cm) 8.5" (21.6 cm)	1" (2.5 cm) 2" (5 cm) 9" (22.9 cm)	1.5" (3.8 cm) 2" (5 cm) 8.5" (21.6 cm)	2.5" (6.4 cm) 3" (7.6 cm) 1.5" (3.8 cm) 1" (2.5 cm) 3.5" (8.9 cm)	5" (12.7 cm) 3" (7.6 cm) 3" (7.6 cm)	12" (30.5 cm)
3" (7.6 cm)	2.5" (6.4 cm)	2" (5 cm)	2.5" (6.4 cm)	1.5" (3.8 cm)	1.5" (3.8 cm)	1.5" (3.8 cm)	2" (5 cm)	2.5" (6.4 cm)	2" (5 cm)

CLASSIC MOJAVE LANDSCAPE

level: beginner/intermediate

Here is the most classic of my landscape styles: the Mojave Desert landscape. This piece was inspired by the rolling hills and sand dunes of this desert, translated into a minimalist abstract art piece. Named after the indigenous Mojave people, this desert is the smallest yet driest of all of the American deserts.

materials

- 5mm string:
    - White: 340 feet (103.6 m)
    - Yellow/mustard: 16.7 feet (5.1 m)
    - Dusty blush: 73.3 feet (22.4 m)
    - Mocha: 73.3 feet (22.4 m)
    - Rust: 85 feet (25.9 m)
- 20-inch (50.8-cm) branch or dowel
- Measuring tape
- Scissors
- Large tapestry needle
- Comb
- Optional: S-hooks and working rack

knots used in this project

- Reverse Lark's Head Knot (page 10)
- Alternating Colors Square Knot Method (page 21)
- Square Knot (page 13)

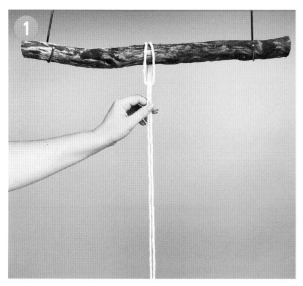

Step 1: Cut 34 white strings into 65-inch (165.1-cm) lengths. Attach all strings to the branch or dowel using a reverse lark's head knot.

Step 2: Cut 17 additional white strings into 110-inch (279.4-cm) lengths. Attach each string to a section of four hanging strings using the alternating colors square knot method. Each section will be referred to as a "column," numbered 1 to 17, from left to right.

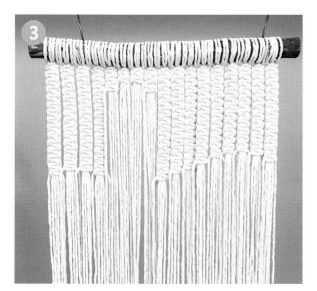

Step 3: Tie continuous square knots down each column according to the lengths in the diagram on page 55.

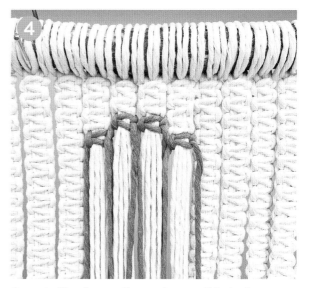

Step 4: Cut four yellow strings to 50-inch (127-cm) lengths to be used for the sun section. Then attach them to columns 5 to 8 using the alternating colors square knot method.

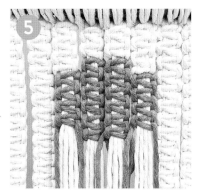

Step 5: Tie continuous yellow square knots down columns 5 to 8 in lengths according to the diagram, tying the knots over all six hanging strings (including the white working cords from the previous section).

Step 6: Once the sun section is complete, switch back to the white working cord by bringing the two white strings in the back to the front and pushing the yellow strings back. Tie square white square knots in columns 5 to 8.

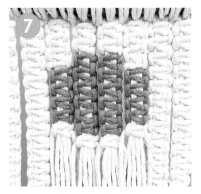

Step 7: Once columns 5 to 8 have white square knots tied, trim off the ends of the yellow strings in the back.

Step 8: Tie continuous white square knots in columns 5 to 8 according to the lengths in the diagram.

Step 9: Cut 11 pieces of blush-colored string to 80-inch (203.2-cm) lengths to be used for the top right layer of hills. Attach to columns 7 to 17 using the alternating colors square knot method.

Step 10: Once all the blush strings are attached with a square knot, trim off the white working cords from the previous section in the back.

Step 11: Tie continuous blush square knots in columns 7 to 17 according to the lengths in the diagram.

Step 12: Cut 11 pieces of mocha-colored string to 80-inch (203.2-cm) lengths to be used for the middle left layer of hills. Attach the strings to columns 1 to 11 using the alternating colors square knot method.

Step 13: Once all the mocha-colored strings are attached, trim the previous working cords off in the back.

Step 14: Tie continuous mocha square knots in columns 1 to 11 according to the lengths in the diagram.

Step 15: Cut 17 rust-colored strings into 60-inch (152.4-cm) lengths for the bottom layer of hills. Attach them to each column using the alternating colors square knot method.

Step 16: Once each rust string is attached, trim off the previous mocha and blush strings in the back.

Step 17: Tie continuous rust square knots according to the lengths in the diagram. Once all columns are finished, make sure the bottoms all end in a straight line across. If any sections need adjustment, add or remove knots until they are even.

Step 18: Flip the piece over to the back. Use a tapestry needle to weave in all loose ends up through the last square knot in the back. Trim off loose strings once woven in.

Step 19: Cut the ends of the hanging strings to the desired length and comb through the strings to create fringe. Trim once more after combing, if needed, to even out the ends.

1	2	3	4	5	6	7	8	9	10	11	12	13	14	15	16	17
				1.5" (3.8 cm)	1" (2.5 cm)	1" (2.5 cm)	1.5" (3.8 cm)									
				2" (5 cm)	3" (7.6 cm)	3" (7.6 cm)	2" (5 cm)									
											6.5" (16.5 cm)	6" (15.2 cm)	6" (15.2 cm)	6" (15.2 cm)	6.5" (16.5 cm)	6.5" (16.5 cm)
										7" (17.8 cm)						
									7.5" (19 cm)							
								8" (20.3 cm)								
8.5" (21.6 cm)	8" (20.3 cm)	8" (20.3 cm)	8" (20.3 cm)	5" (12.7 cm)			5" (12.7 cm)									
					5" (12.7 cm)	5" (12.7 cm)										
						0.5" (1.3 cm)	1.5" (3.8 cm)									
								2.5" (6.4 cm)								
									3.5" (8.9 cm)							
										4.5" (11.4 cm)	5" (12.7 cm)	5.5" (14 cm)				
													6" (15.2 cm)	6" (15.2 cm)		
							2.5" (6.4 cm)	2" (5 cm)	1" (2.5 cm)						6" (15.2 cm)	
	5" (12.7 cm)	5" (12.7 cm)														6.5" (16.5 cm)
5" (12.7 cm)			5.5" (14 cm)	5" (12.7 cm)	4" (10.2 cm)	3.5" (8.9 cm)										
2.5" (6.4 cm)	3" (7.6 cm)	3" (7.6 cm)	2.5" (6.4 cm)	2.5" (6.4 cm)	3" (7.6 cm)	3" (7.6 cm)	3.5" (8.9 cm)	3.5" (8.9 cm)	4" (10.2 cm)	4.5" (11.4 cm)	4.5" (11.4 cm)	4.5" (11.4 cm)	4" (10.2 cm)	4" (10.2 cm)	3.5" (8.9 cm)	3" (7.6 cm)

SEDONA LANDSCAPE

level: beginner/intermediate

Have you ever heard of vortexes? A vortex is thought to be a swirling center of energy in the earth. These sites are believed to be healing and meditative, and Sedona draws visitors from all around the world hoping to experience this energy in one of their many vortexes. Aside from its mystical energy, Sedona has a uniquely stunning desertscape. Red rock formations are contrasted by lush green forest for an epic view all around, which I've tried to recreate in this piece.

materials

- 5mm string:
  - White: 326 feet (99.4 m)
  - Yellow/mustard: 16.7 feet (5.1 m)
  - Rust: 156 feet (47.5 m)
  - Sage: 68.7 feet (20.9 m)
  - Pine: 68.7 feet (20.9 m)
- 20-inch (50.8-cm) branch or dowel
- Measuring tape
- Scissors
- Large tapestry needle
- Comb
- Optional: S-hooks and working rack

knots used in this project

- Reverse Lark's Head Knot (page 10)
- Alternating Colors Square Knot Method (page 21)
- Square Knot (page 13)

Step 2: Cut 17 additional white strings into 110-inch (279.4-cm) lengths. Attach each new white string to a section of four hanging cords using the alternating colors square knot method. Each section will be referred to as a "column," numbered 1 to 17, from left to right.

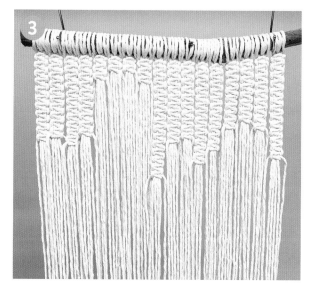

Step 1: Cut 34 white strings into 60-inch (152.4-cm) lengths. Attach all 34 strings to the branch using a reverse lark's head knot.

Step 3: Tie continuous white square knots down each column according to the lengths in the diagram on page 62.

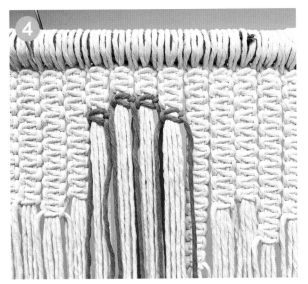

Step 4: Cut four yellow strings into 50-inch (127-cm) lengths to be used for the sun section. Then, attach them to columns 5 to 8 using the alternating colors square knot method.

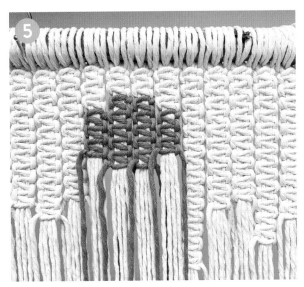

Step 5: Tie continuous yellow square knots to create the sun shape according to the lengths in the diagram, making sure to tie the yellow string over all six hanging strings (including the white working cords from the previous section).

Step 6: Once the sun section is complete, alternate columns 5 to 8 back to the white working cords by bringing the two white strings forward while pushing the yellow strings to the back. Tie a white square knot over all other strings in each column.

Step 7: Trim off the ends of the yellow strings in the back once a white square knot has been added to columns 5 to 8.

Step 8: Tie continuous white square knots in columns 5 to 8 according to the lengths in the diagram.

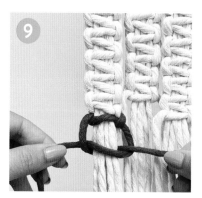

Step 9: Cut 17 pieces of rust-colored string into 110-inch (279.4-cm) lengths to be used for the red rocks section. Attach them under the white cords using the alternating colors square knot method.

Step 10: Once all the rust strings are attached using one square knot, trim off the previous white working cords in the back.

Step 11: Tie continuous rust square knots down each column according to the lengths in the diagram.

Step 12: Cut 15 pieces of sage-colored string into 55-inch (139.7-cm) lengths to be used for the grassy ground section. Attach them to columns 3 to 17 using the alternating colors square knot method.

Step 13: Once the sage-colored strings are attached, trim off the working cords from the previous section in the back.

Step 14: Tie continuous square knots using the sage string in lengths according to the diagram.

Step 15: Cut 15 pieces of pine-colored string into 55-inch (139.7-cm) lengths to be used for the tree and brush section. Attach them to columns 1 to 9 and 12 to 17 using the alternating colors square knot method.

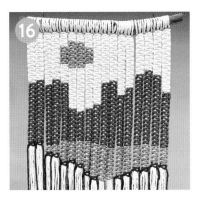

Step 16: Trim off the working cords from the previous sections in the back of columns 1 to 9 and 12 to 17.

Step 17: Tie continuous pine square knots according to the lengths in the diagram. Once all the square knots are complete, make sure that all the columns end in a relatively straight line at the bottom. Make adjustments if needed by adding or removing knots.

Step 18: Flip the piece over to the back. Use a tapestry needle to weave the loose ends at the bottom of each column upward through the last square knot. Pull the strings all the way through and trim off the loose ends.

Step 19: Trim the hanging strings to the desired length and brush out with a comb to create fringe. After combing, go through and trim the fringe one more time, if needed.

1	2	3	4	5	6	7	8	9	10	11	12	13	14	15	16	17
				1.5" (3.8 cm)	1" (2.5 cm)	1" (2.5 cm)	1.5" (3.8 cm)									
				2" (5 cm)	3" (7.6 cm)	3" (7.6 cm)	2" (5 cm)									
5" (12.7 cm)	5" (12.7 cm)												5" (12.7 cm)	4.5" (11.4 cm)	5" (12.7 cm)	
		6" (15.2 cm)	5.5" (14 cm)	2.5" (6.4 cm)					6" (15.2 cm)	6" (15.2 cm)						6" (15.2 cm)
											7.5" (19 cm)	7" (17.8 cm)				
					5" (12.7 cm)		5.5" (14 cm)	8.5" (21.6 cm)								
						5.5" (14 cm)										
7" (17.8 cm)	7" (17.8 cm)	6" (15.2 cm)	7" (17.8 cm)	6.5" (16.5 cm)	3.5" (8.9 cm)					6.5" (16.5 cm)	5" (12.7 cm)	5.5" (14 cm)	7" (17.8 cm)	7.5" (19 cm)	7" (17.8 cm)	6.5" (16.5 cm)
						3.5" (8.9 cm)	4" (10.2 cm)	4.5" (11.4 cm)	7" (17.8 cm)							
		1" (2.5 cm)	1" (2.5 cm)							4" (10.2 cm)						
				2" (5 cm)	1.5" (3.8 cm)										2.5" (6.4 cm)	
						2" (5 cm)	2.5" (6.4 cm)					3" (7.6 cm)	3" (7.6 cm)	3" (7.6 cm)		2.5" (6.4 cm)
4.5" (11.4 cm)	4.5" (11.4 cm)	3.5" (8.9 cm)	3" (7.6 cm)	2" (5 cm)	2.5" (6.4 cm)	1.5" (3.8 cm)	1" (2.5 cm)	3" (7.6 cm)	3.5" (8.9 cm)	4" (10.2 cm)	3.5" (8.9 cm)	1" (2.5 cm)	1.5" (3.8 cm)	1.5" (3.8 cm)	2" (5 cm)	1.5" (3.8 cm)
								0.5" (1.3 cm)			0.5" (1.3 cm)					

SONORA TASSEL WALL HANGING

level: advanced

This piece is the best of both worlds—the abstract and minimalist style of classic landscape designs mixed with tassels and some boho flair for a more layered macramé shape. The central focal point of this desert landscape piece paired with intricate clove hitch knot patterns and multiple layers make this a more advanced wall hanging. Before you start, I recommend practicing the diagonal clove hitch knot to build up muscle memory.

materials

- 5mm string:
  - White: 580 feet (176.8 m)
  - Yellow/mustard: 12.5 feet (3.8 m)
  - Rust: 87.5 feet (26.7 m)
  - Dusty blush: 40 feet (12.2 m)
- 29-inch (73.7-cm) branch or dowel
- Measuring tape
- Scissors
- Comb
- Optional: Tapestry needle, S-hooks, and working rack

knots used in this project

- Reverse Lark's Head Knot (page 10)
- Alternating Colors Square Knot Method (page 21)
- Square Knot (page 13)
- Diagonal Clove Hitch Knot (page 15)
- Gathering Knot (page 18)
- Lark's Head Knot (page 10)
- Rya Knot (page 20)

layer 1

Step 1: Cut 16 pieces of white string into 80-inch (203.2-cm) lengths. Attach them to the center of the branch or dowel using a reverse lark's head knot.

Step 2: Cut eight additional pieces of white string into 50-inch (127-cm) lengths. Attach each string to a section of four hanging strings using the alternating colors square knot method. Each section will be referred to as a "column," numbered 1 to 8, from left to right.

Step 3: Tie continuous white square knots down each column according to the lengths in the diagram on page 71.

Step 4: Cut three yellow strings into 50-inch (127-cm) lengths for the sun section. Attach the yellow strings to columns 2 to 4 using the alternating colors square knot method.

Step 5: Tie continuous yellow square knots according to the lengths in the diagram. Be sure to tie each yellow square knot over all six white strings, including the previous white working cords.

Step 6: Bring the white working cords from the previous section forward, and push the yellow strings to the back. Tie white square knots in columns 2 to 4 using the alternating colors square knot method.

Step 7: Trim off the yellow strings in the back, then tie continuous white square knots according to the lengths in the diagram.

Step 8: Cut five pieces of rust string into 80-inch (203.2-cm) lengths for the top right hill layer. Attach them to columns 4 to 8 using the alternating colors square knot method.

Step 9: Trim off the white strings in the back once the rust strings are attached, and then tie continuous rust square knots according to the lengths in the diagram.

Step 10: Cut six pieces of blush string into 80-inch (203.2-cm) lengths for the lower left hill layer. Attach the blush strings to columns 1 to 6 using the alternating colors square knot method.

Step 11: Trim off the working cords from the previous sections for columns 1 to 6, then tie continuous blush square knots according to the lengths in the diagram. Optional: Use a tapestry needle to weave in the ends of the working cords.

layer 2

Step 12: Cut six white strings into 12-foot (3.7-m) lengths. Divide them into two groups of three strings, and use reverse lark's head knots to attach each group to the branch approximately 2 inches (5 cm) out from layer 1.

Step 13: Starting on one side at a time, take the center two strings and cross one over the other. Use the string that is underneath to tie a diagonal clove hitch knot. Both of these strings will be used as lead cords to create the top half of a diamond shape.

Step 14: Continue using the same lead cord from the previous step and tie a row of diagonal clove hitch knots with the remaining two strings on the right.

Step 15: Pick up the first working cord from the row of diagonal clove hitch knots just tied, then direct it diagonally to the right to function as the lead cord for the next row.

Step 16: Use the two strings on the left to tie diagonal clove hitch knots around the lead cord. This will result in an inverted "V" shape.

Step 17: Tie a square knot in the middle using the center four cords.

Step 18: Using the same lead cords as before, direct both inward and tie rows of diagonal clove hitch knots to create a "V" shape.

Step 19: At the bottom of the "V," cross one lead cord over the other and tie a diagonal clove hitch knot.

Step 20: Continue tying diamond patterns until you have created six full diamonds.

Step 21: Repeat the diamond pattern on the other side, creating six full diamonds.

Step 22: Bring both sections together in the center. Use the innermost three strings from each diamond to create a new diamond, joining both sides together.

Step 23: Cut 24 white strings into 50-inch (127-cm) lengths. Attach the strings using a reverse lark's head knot to the outer string from each diamond pattern, in groups of two strings in each section.

layer 3

Step 24: Cut four pieces of white string into 9-foot (2.7-m) lengths. Divide them into two groups of two strings each, then attach each group about 2 inches (5 cm) out from the last layer using a reverse lark's head knot.

Step 25: Cut two pieces of rust-colored string into 15-foot (4.6-m) lengths. Attach each rust string to one of the groups of white string using the alternating colors square knot method.

Step 26: Tie continuous rust square knots on both sides until they are about 17 inches (43.2 cm) long each.

Step 27: Gather both sections in the center. Cut one more rust string to 30 inches (76.2 cm) long and use it to tie a gathering knot around both groups of string. Trim off the excess string from the top of the gathering knot.

layer 4

Step 28: Cut eight white strings into 15-foot (4.6-m) lengths. Divide the strings into two groups of four strings each, then attach each group to the branch approximately 2 inches (5 cm) out from the last section using a reverse lark's head knot.

Step 29: Use diagonal clove hitch knots and square knots to create the same diamond pattern for this section as in layer 2 (however, these diamonds will have one extra string on each side because they are groups of four strings instead of the three that were used in layer 2).

Step 30: Create eight large diamond designs on each side.

Step 31: Connect both sections in the center by using the four inner cords from each section to create another diamond.

Step 32: Cut 48 pieces of white string into 28-inch (71-cm) lengths. Attach them in groups of three to the outer string from each diamond pattern using a reverse lark's head knot.

Step 33: Trim all of the bottom fringe into a "V" shape.

Step 34: Cut 18 pieces of rust-colored string to 14-inch (35.6-cm) lengths. Take two strings at a time and attach them using a lark's head knot on the strings just above where the white fringe was attached.

Step 35: Use a rya knot to attach the last pair of rust strings to the bottom of the center diamond.

1	2	3	4	5	6	7	8
		0.5" (1.3 cm)					
	1" (2.5 cm)		1" (2.5 cm)				
	1.5" (3.8 cm)	2.5" (6.4 cm)	1.5" (3.8 cm)				
					3.5" (8.9 cm)	3.5" (8.9 cm)	
4.5" (11.4 cm)				4.5" (11.4 cm)			4" (10.2 cm)
	1.5" (3.8 cm)	1.5" (3.8 cm)	2" (5 cm)				
			0.5" (1.3 cm)				
					2" (5 cm)		
2.5" (6.4 cm)					3.5" (8.9 cm)		3" (7.6 cm)
	3.5" (8.9 cm)					4" (10 cm)	
		3.5" (8.9 cm)					
			3.5" (8.9 cm)	2.5" (6.4 cm)	1" (2.5 cm)		

Step 36: Use a comb to brush out the rust tassels, then trim each tassel to 3 inches (7.6 cm) in length.

MOUNTAIN AND FOREST

Nothing reminds me of how infinitely small I am more than standing in a thick forest full of giant trees or at the top of a mountain range, looking out as far as the eye can see. But feeling small isn't always a bad thing—it can be both freeing and humbling. Forests and mountains also bring us a sense of adventure, giving us the opportunity to explore and be challenged by Mother Nature in the most authentic way. Whether you are standing at the top of the world or shifting your perspective down to all of the intriguing objects that cover the forest floor, there is never a shortage of beauty and inspiration in the mountains.

The next several projects capture both the intricacies of the forest and the majesty of an epic mountain viewpoint. We will create tiny mushroom habitats, charming leafy vines, and layered mountain landscapes. This chapter also contains a larger variety of project difficulties and knotting techniques to keep you on your toes.

PONDEROSA PLANT HANGER

level: beginner

This nature-inspired project is subtle and sophisticated; from afar, it may just look like a classic plant hanger. But up close, the details of the pine-shaped trees come to life and bring a foresty element forward. This pine tree pattern could easily be translated into other designs for wall hangings and more!

materials

- 5mm pine-colored string: 149 feet (45.4 m)
- 2-inch (5-cm) wooden ring
- Measuring tape
- Scissors
- Optional: S-hook and working rack

knots used in this project

- Gathering Knot (page 18)
- Square Knot (page 13)
- Diagonal Clove Hitch Knot (page 15)

Step 1: Cut 12 lengths of string into 12-foot (3.7-m) lengths. Feed all 12 strings through the wooden ring so that they hang evenly on both sides.

Step 2: Cut another string to 30 inches (76.2 cm) in length. Use this string to tie a gathering knot underneath the ring, wrapping around approximately five times before securing.

Step 3: Trim off both loose strings from the top and the bottom of the gathering knot.

Step 4: Separate all of the hanging strings into three groups of eight strings each. Start with one group and move the other groups out of the way for now.

Step 5: Use the two outer strings in this group to tie a square knot around the six remaining strings. Tie this square knot directly underneath the gathering knot.

Step 6: Use the center two strings to tie a single diagonal clove hitch knot approximately 2 inches (5 cm) underneath the square knot from the previous step. These two strings will be used as lead cords for the next step.

Step 7: Use the next two strings over (one on each side of the first clove hitch knot) to tie two additional diagonal clove hitch knots downward at a diagonal angle. This will create an inverted "V" shape.

Step 8: Return to the center two cords and tie another clove hitch knot. Use these two strings as lead cords for the next step.

Step 9: Tie two more diagonal clove hitch knots around the lead cords on either side. This will create a slightly longer inverted "V" shape below the first one.

Step 10: Returning to the center two strings again for a new row, create a third inverted "V" using the same method. For this row, add on an extra knot on each side so that all eight strings have been tied.

Step 11: Repeat step 10 for one additional row so that there are four rows of diagonal clove hitch knots.

Step 12: Use the four center strings to tie two consecutive square knots. This completes one pine tree pattern.

Step 13: Measure approximately 2 inches (5 cm) below the bottom of the first tree and use the outer two strings to tie a square knot around the inner six strings.

Step 14: Repeat steps 5 to 13 for the other two groups of eight strings.

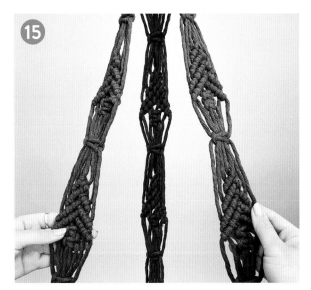

Step 15: Starting another 2 inches (5 cm) down from the last square knot in each section, repeat the same tree and square knot pattern (steps 6 to 13) until each group has three pine tree patterns, each separated by a square knot.

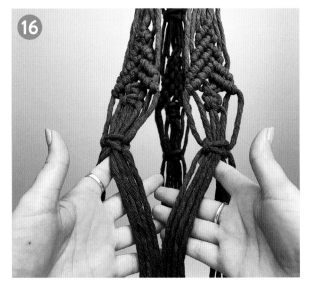

Step 16: Once all the sections are complete, take two sections that are next to each other and join four strings from one with four strings from another to create a new group of eight strings.

Step 17: Using the new groups of eight strings, tie square knots with the outer two strings approximately 3 inches (7.6 cm) below the last square knots. Repeat until all three new groups of strings have been tied into square knots.

Step 18: Cut another string to 30 inches (76.2 cm) in length. Use it to tie a gathering knot approximately 3 inches (7.6 cm) below the last square knots. Wrap the gathering knot around all strings approximately five times before securing.

Step 19: Trim the top string off from the gathering knot, then trim all string ends to the desired length.

BEYOND THE PINES LANDSCAPE

level: beginner

Have you ever heard of "forest bathing"? The concept originated from the Japanese phrase *shinrin-yoku* that gained popularity in the 1980s. It is the physiological and psychological exercise of walking through the woods and taking in the atmosphere. The act of immersing oneself in all the sights, smells, and sounds of the forest has extremely healing benefits for the mind and body, such as lowering blood pressure and stress hormones. Macramé can also be an incredible activity for mindfulness—try practicing some presence and meditation as you make this piece!

materials

- 5mm string:
  - White: 237.5 feet (72.4 m)
  - Yellow/mustard: 16.7 feet (5.1 m)
  - Sage: 162.5 feet (49.5 m)
  - Pine: 80 feet (24.4 m)
- 17-inch (43.2-cm) branch or dowel
- Measuring tape
- Scissors
- Large tapestry needle
- Comb
- Optional: S-hooks and working rack

knots used in this project

- Reverse Lark's Head Knot (page 10)
- Alternating Colors Square Knot Method (page 21)
- Square Knot (page 13)
- Square Knot Picot (page 14)

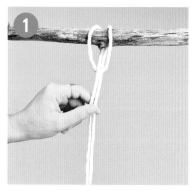

Step 1: Cut 30 pieces of white string into 55-inch (139.7-cm) lengths. Attach all 30 pieces to the branch using a reverse lark's head knot.

Step 2: Cut 15 pieces of white string into 80-inch (203.2-cm) lengths. Attach each white string over a section of four hanging lead strings using the alternating colors square knot method. Each group of strings will be referred to as a "column," numbered 1 to 15, from left to right.

Step 3: Tie continuous white square knots down each column according to the lengths in the diagram on page 85.

Step 4: Cut four pieces of yellow string to 50-inch (127-cm) lengths for the sun section. Use the alternating colors square knot method to attach the yellow strings to columns 10 to 13.

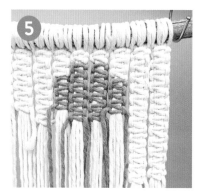

Step 5: Tie continuous yellow square knots down columns 10 to 13 in lengths according to the diagram. Be sure to tie the yellow string over all six white cords, including the previous white working cords in the back.

Step 6: After the yellow section is complete, take the two white working cords from the back of each column and bring them to the front, while pushing the yellow working cords to the back. Use the white strings to tie a square knot over all the strings.

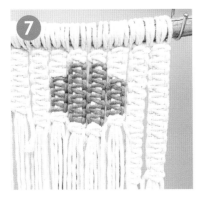

Step 7: Once columns 10 to 13 have a white square knot, trim off the loose ends of the yellow strings in the back.

Step 8: Tie continuous square knots in columns 10 to 13 using the white string according to the lengths shown in the diagram.

Step 9: Cut 15 sage strings to 130-inch (330.2-cm) lengths for the mountain backdrop section. Attach a sage-colored string to each column using the alternating colors square knot method.

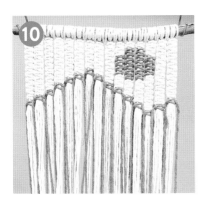

Step 10: Once each sage string is attached with a square knot, trim off the white working cords from the previous section in the back.

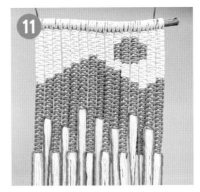

Step 11: Tie continuous square knots using the sage string in lengths according to the diagram.

Step 12: Cut eight pine-colored strings into 120-inch (304.8-cm) lengths for the tree line section. Attach the pine strings to columns 2, 4, 6, 8, 10, 12, and 14 using the alternating colors square knot method.

Step 13: Once the pine strings are attached, trim off the previous sage working cords in the back.

Step 14: Working in one column at a time, tie a square knot picot about 0.5 inch (1.3 cm) or so below the first square knot.

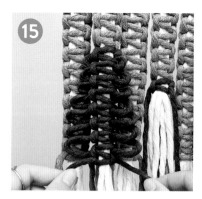

Step 15: Continue tying square knot picots down each column, leaving a slightly larger space between each knot from the previous one. This will gradually increase the size of the loops, creating a triangular "pine tree" shape.

Step 16: Continue tying pine-colored square knot picots down all even-numbered columns until the bottom of all the columns are even. If needed, add or untie any knots to even out the bottom.

Step 17: Flip the piece over to the back. Thread the loose ends of each string through the eye of the tapestry needle and weave upward, underneath the last square knot, to secure it. Repeat with each column and then trim all the loose ends.

Step 18: Flip the piece back over to the front and trim to the desired length. Then, use a comb to gently brush out the hanging strings from the bottom upward. Once all the fringe is combed, give the bottom a final trim to even out the ends.

1	2	3	4	5	6	7	8	9	10	11	12	13	14	15
										0.5" (1.3 cm)	0.5" (1.3 cm)			
									1" (2.5 cm)			1" (2.5 cm)		
									2" (5 cm)	3" (7.6 cm)	3" (7.6 cm)	2" (5 cm)		
				4" (10.2 cm)	3.5" (8.9 cm)	3" (7.6 cm)	3.5" (8.9 cm)	4" (10.2 cm)						5" (12.7 cm)
			4.5" (11.4 cm)						1.5" (3.8 cm)					
6" (15.2 cm)	5.5" (14 cm)	5" (12.7 cm)								1.5" (3.8 cm)	2" (5 cm)	5.5" (14 cm)	
												3" (7.6 cm)		
					5.5" (14 cm)									
	4.5" (11.4 cm)						6.5" (16.5 cm)				4" (10.2 cm)		5" (12.7 cm)	
			6.5" (16.5 cm)						6.5" (16.5 cm)					
8" (20.3 cm)	4" (10.2 cm)	9" (22.9 cm)	3" (7.6 cm)	10" (25.4 cm)	5" (12.7 cm)	11" (28 cm)	4" (10.2 cm)	10" (25.4 cm)	3" (7.6 cm)	9" (22.9 cm)	4.5" (11.4 cm)	8" (20.3 cm)	3.5" (8.9 cm)	9" (22.9 cm)

CASCADE MOUNTAIN LANDSCAPE

level: beginner/intermediate

Famous mountaineer John Muir once said, "The clearest way into the Universe is through a forest wilderness." There is something so refreshing about journeying into the mountains. Nature has its way of reminding us how infinitely small we are when we get to the top of a mountain and look out at the vast expanse and layers of mountains cascading upon each other. While a wall hanging isn't quite as magnificent as looking at the real thing, it serves as a beautiful representative of that breathtaking feeling.

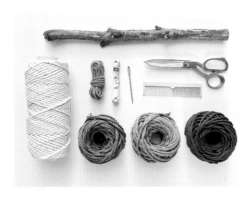

materials

- 5mm string:
  - White: 216.7 feet (66 m)
  - Yellow/mustard: 8.3 feet (2.5 m)
  - Sage: 86.7 feet (26.4 m)
  - Teal: 86.7 feet (26.4 m)
  - Pine: 86.7 feet (26.4 m)
- 17-inch (43.2-cm) branch or dowel
- Measuring tape
- Scissors
- Large tapestry needle
- Comb
- Optional: S-hooks and working rack

knots used in this project

- Reverse Lark's Head Knot (page 10)
- Alternating Colors Square Knot Method (page 21)
- Square Knot (page 13)

Step 1: Cut 26 pieces of white string into 60-inch (152.4-cm) lengths. Attach all 26 pieces to the branch using a reverse lark's head knot.

Step 2: Cut 13 additional pieces of white string into 80-inch (203.2-cm) lengths. Attach each white string over a section of four hanging strings using the alternating colors square knot method. Each section will be referred to as a "column," numbered 1 to 13, from left to right.

Step 3: Tie continuous white square knots down each column according to the lengths in the diagram on page 91.

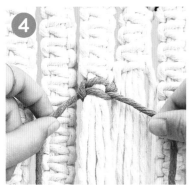

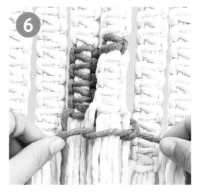

Step 4: Cut two pieces of yellow string into 50-inch (127-cm) lengths for the moon section. Use the alternating colors square knot method to attach these two strings to columns 9 and 10. Be sure to knot the yellow strings on top of all strings, including the previous white working cords.

Step 5: In column 9, tie continuous square knots according to the lengths in the diagram. For column 10, tie a single square knot before switching back to the white strings from the last section.

Step 6: Tie 1.5 inches (3.8 cm) of white square knots in column 10. Then, alternate back to the yellow string and tie one more yellow square knot.

Step 7: In columns 9 and 10, alternate back to the white string and then trim off the yellow strings in the back. Tie continuous white square knots according to the diagram.

Step 8: Cut 13 sage-colored strings into 80-inch (203.2-cm) lengths for the top layer of mountains. Attach them to all the columns using the alternating colors square knot method.

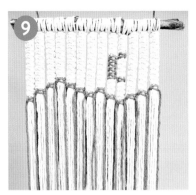

Step 9: Once all the sage-colored strings are attached, trim off the white working cords from the previous section in the back.

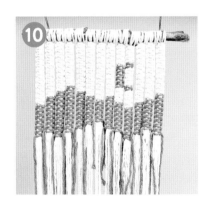

Step 10: Tie continuous sage square knots according to the lengths in the diagram.

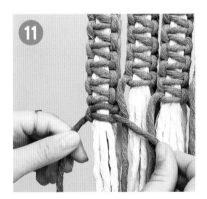

Step 11: Cut 13 teal strings into 80-inch (203.2-cm) lengths for the middle layer of mountains. Attach them to each column using the alternating colors square knot method.

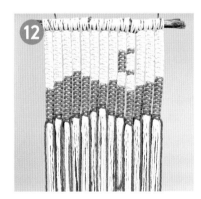

Step 12: Once all the teal-colored strings are attached, trim off the sage working cords from the previous section in the back.

Step 13: Tie continuous teal square knots according to the lengths in the diagram.

Step 14: Cut 13 pine-colored strings into 80-inch (203.2-cm) lengths for the bottom layer of mountains. Attach them to each column using the alternating colors square knot method.

Step 15: Once all the pine-colored strings are attached, trim off the teal strings from the previous section in the back.

Step 16: Tie continuous pine square knots according to the lengths in the diagram. All ends should form an even line across the bottom; add or remove knots if needed to even out the line.

Step 17: Flip the tapestry over to the back. Use the tapestry needle to weave the loose ends of the pine-colored string upward through the last square knot. Repeat for each column, then trim off the loose ends.

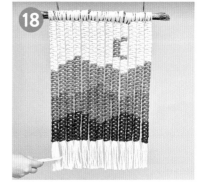

Step 18: Trim the hanging cords to the desired length, then comb through to create fluffy fringe. If needed, trim one more time to even out the ends.

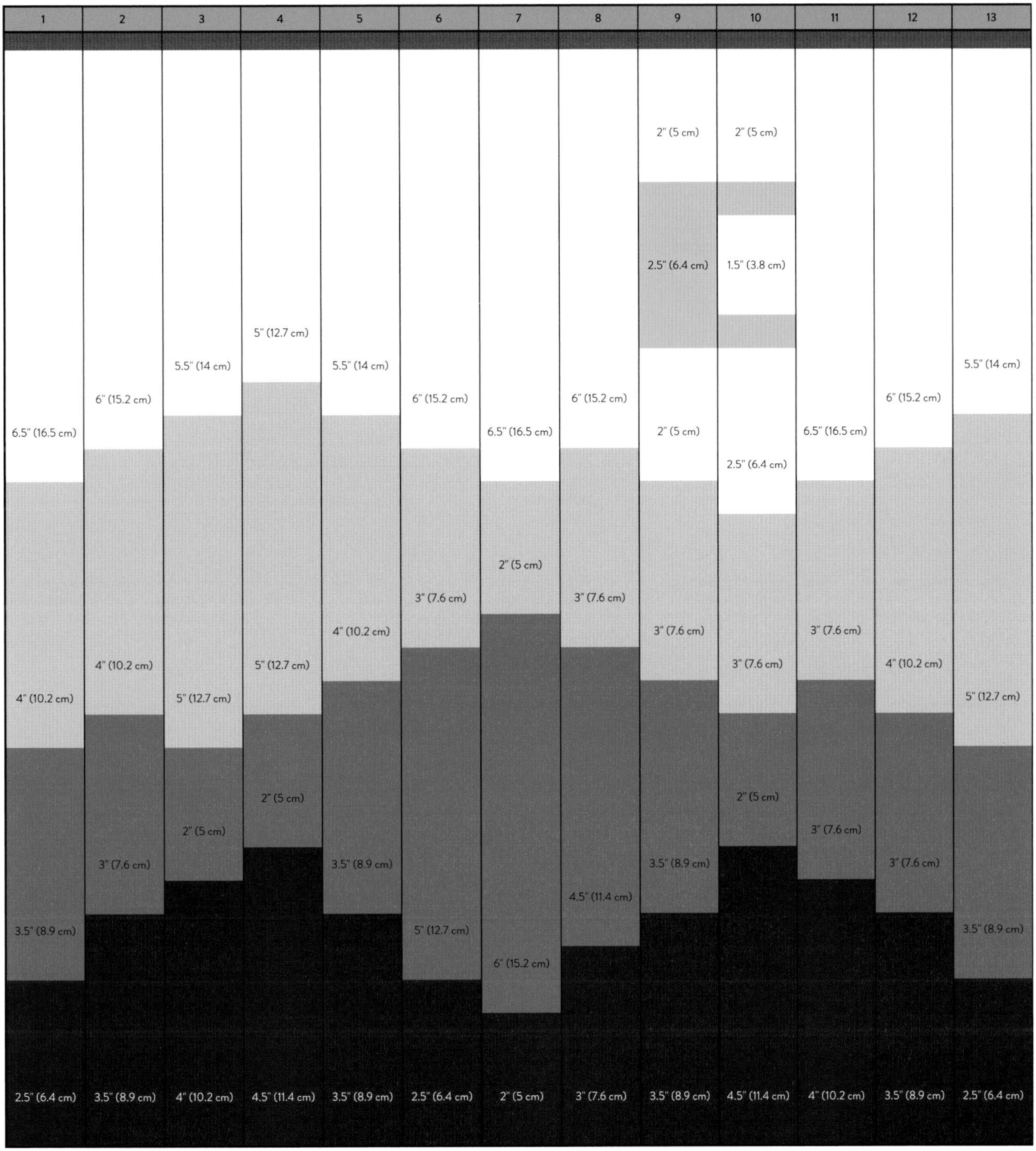

1
6.5" (16.5 cm)
4" (10.2 cm)
3.5" (8.9 cm)
2.5" (6.4 cm)
2
6" (15.2 cm)
4" (10.2 cm)
3" (7.6 cm)
3.5" (8.9 cm)
3
5.5" (14 cm)
5" (12.7 cm)
2" (5 cm)
4" (10.2 cm)
4
5" (12.7 cm)
5" (12.7 cm)
2" (5 cm)
4.5" (11.4 cm)
5
5.5" (14 cm)
4" (10.2 cm)
3.5" (8.9 cm)
3.5" (8.9 cm)
6
6" (15.2 cm)
3" (7.6 cm)
5" (12.7 cm)
2.5" (6.4 cm)
7
6.5" (16.5 cm)
2" (5 cm)
6" (15.2 cm)
2" (5 cm)
8
6" (15.2 cm)
3" (7.6 cm)
4.5" (11.4 cm)
3" (7.6 cm)
9
2" (5 cm)
2.5" (6.4 cm)
2" (5 cm)
3" (7.6 cm)
3.5" (8.9 cm)
3.5" (8.9 cm)
10
2" (5 cm)
1.5" (3.8 cm)
2.5" (6.4 cm)
3" (7.6 cm)
2" (5 cm)
4.5" (11.4 cm)
11
6.5" (16.5 cm)
3" (7.6 cm)
3" (7.6 cm)
4" (10.2 cm)
12
6" (15.2 cm)
4" (10.2 cm)
3" (7.6 cm)
3.5" (8.9 cm)
13
5.5" (14 cm)
5" (12.7 cm)
3.5" (8.9 cm)
2.5" (6.4 cm)

MUSHROOM GARDEN HOOP

level: intermediate

Dip your toes into the world of sculptural macramé, and create a mini mushroom garden that any fairy would be proud to call home. Clove hitch knots will be used to create three-dimensional mushrooms that pop right out of the vine-framed hoop. Sculptural macramé is more challenging because uneven tension in the knots can create lopsided variances in the shape or structure. This project is best attempted once you are very familiar with the clove hitch knot and able to maintain consistent tension.

materials

- 3mm string:
  - Sage: 38.3 feet (11.7 m)
  - Mocha: 58.3 feet (17.8 m)
  - White: 56.7 feet (17.3 m)
  - Rust: 58.3 feet (17.8 m)
- 5-inch (12.7-cm) metal hoop or frame
- Measuring tape
- Scissors
- Tapestry needle

knots used in this project

- Lark's Head Knot (page 10)
- Single Strand Lark's Head Knot (page 11)
- Reverse Lark's Head Knot (page 10)
- Diagonal Clove Hitch Knot (page 15)
- Horizontal Clove Hitch Knot (page 16)
- Gathering Knot (page 18)

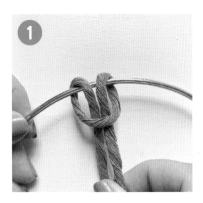

part 1: leaves and vine

Step 1: Cut one sage-colored string to 100 inches (254 cm) in length. Attach it to the hoop using a lark's head knot, leaving approximately 5 inches (12.7 cm) of string loose on one side and all of the remaining length on the other side.

Step 2: Use the longer side of the string to tie continuous single strand lark's head knots along the hoop.

Step 3: Continue tying single strand lark's head knots until you have knotted over about two-thirds of the hoop; there should only be about 6 inches (15.2 cm) of space at the bottom of the hoop that is left bare.

Step 4: Cut six more sage-colored strings into 60-inch (152.4-cm) lengths for the leaves. Attach three of those strings underneath where the last section ends on the left using reverse lark's head knots.

Step 5: Take the first string from the bottom and cross it up over the other five strings. Use this string as a lead cord and tie a row of five diagonal clove hitch knots around it with the other strings.

Step 6: Pick up the second string from the bottom and cross it up over the remaining four strings; using it as a lead cord, tie the next row of diagonal clove hitch knots.

Step 7: After tying the second row, pick up the third string from the bottom and cross it up over the remaining three strings. Use this as the lead cord and tie the next row of diagonal clove hitch knots.

Step 8: Take the fourth string and cross it over the last two strings; use this as a lead cord and tie the last row of two diagonal clove hitch knots.

Step 9: Now the first half of the leaf is complete and the clove hitch knots will be reversed in direction to complete the leaf.

Step 10: Take the top string and direct it back down toward the base of the leaf. Use this as a lead cord and tie two diagonal clove hitch knots with the next two strings.

Step 11: Grab the string that is now at the top and direct it down toward the base of the leaf. Use this as a lead cord to tie another row of three diagonal clove hitch knots.

Step 12: After tying the last row, pick up the string now on top and direct it toward the base of the leaf. Tie another row of four diagonal clove hitch knots.

Step 13: Grab the new top string, directing it toward the base of the leaf again. Use this to tie the final row of five diagonal clove hitch knots.

NOTE: As you tie each knot in this row, gather the strings from the previous knots with the lead cord, tying each clove hitch over both the original lead cord and the previous working cord(s).

Step 14: Once the last row is complete, take the last working cord and use it to tie a clove hitch knot around the hoop to secure the leaf.

Step 15: Flip the piece over to the back and thread the loose string that was wrapped around the hoop in steps 1 to 3 through the tapestry needle. Use the needle to pull the loose string through one of the knots on the back of the leaf. After securing it, trim off the excess string.

Step 16: Mirror the same leaf pattern on the other side of the hoop, starting with step 4 and going in the opposite direction, to create one more leaf.

part 2: mushrooms

Step 17: Cut 10 pieces of mocha string and four pieces of white string to 70-inch (177.8-cm) lengths. Take one of the mocha strings and fold it in half; this will be the lead cord through the whole mushroom cap.

Step 18: Attach two additional mocha strings to the center of the first string using a reverse lark's head knot.

Step 19: Take one end of the lead cord and cross it over the other.

Step 20: Use the string underneath to tie a clove hitch knot around the string crossed on top. Tie the knot tight so that no extra string is showing and it resembles a somewhat round shape.

Step 21: Find the lead cord from the last clove hitch knot; moving forward, all other knots and all new strings will be attached around it.

Step 22: Attach a white string to the lead cord using a reverse lark's head knot.

Step 23: Tie two horizontal clove hitch knots around the lead cord using the next two mocha strings.

Step 24: Attach another mocha string to fill the gap using a reverse lark's head knot.

Step 25: Pick up the pattern so far and use your pointer finger to push upward from the bottom, so that the knots start to form an inverted bowl shape. Do this periodically while tying knots to help the mushroom cap form its shape. Continue tying horizontal clove hitch knots using the mocha string, or adding extra string wherever there is a gap.

Step 26: When tying a new row directly underneath where the white strings were previously attached, do not use the white strings to tie clove hitch knots. Instead, tuck the white strings underneath and push them to the inside. Then, attach one or two mocha strings in its place with reverse lark's head knots.

Step 27: Continue tying horizontal clove hitch knots, adding new strings wherever there is a gap between knots. Add in white strings periodically instead of mocha wherever you would like there to be a spot on the mushroom.

Step 28: Once all the precut strings are attached and you are happy with the size and shape of the mushroom, you can stop tying clove hitch knots. The mushrooms in this sample are just over 1 inch (2.5 cm) long for size reference.

Step 29: Cut one white string to 60 inches (152.4 cm). Determine which side of the mushroom should be in the back, and tie a gathering knot to form the stem on that side.

Step 30: Once the gathering knot is complete, trim off the top and bottom strings. Then gently pull each string on the bottom, one at a time, to make sure that no loose strings are showing above the stem.

Step 31: Repeat Steps 17 to 30 with the rust-colored cord to make a second mushroom. Some ways to change the shape or size of the second mushroom include adding extra strings, adjusting the tension of the knots, or creating a longer or shorter stem with the gathering knot.

Step 32: Place the mushrooms over the hoop and determine their ideal placement.

Step 33: Take the bottom strings of each mushroom and divide them in half, into front and back sections. Place the back section behind the hoop.

Step 34: Use strings from the front and back sections, and tie simple overhand knots around the hoop tightly. Tie four or five knots along the bottom of each mushroom to secure it in place.

Step 35: Trim the bottom strings to the desired shape and length.

IVY WALL HANGING

level: advanced

Ivy is a fascinating plant. It is an evergreen vine that can grow in even the harshest conditions. It is often used to symbolize eternity and fidelity across different cultures. Some types of ivy can be toxic, while others are healing and medicinal. This wall hanging is a way to capture the beauty of the ivy plant in another evergreen art form: macramé.

This project will be more challenging because of the multiple layers. Using clove hitch knots to create the vine patterns will require some finesse and attention to detail as well.

materials

- 5mm pine-colored string: 650 feet (198.1 m)
- 30-inch (76.2-cm) branch or dowel
- Measuring tape
- Scissors
- Optional: S-hooks and working rack

knots used in this project

- Reverse Lark's Head Knot (page 10)
- Diagonal Clove Hitch Knot (page 15)
- Gathering Knot (page 18)
- Square Knot (page 13)

layer 1

Step 1: Cut 15 pieces of string into 11-foot (3.4-m) lengths. Attach all strings to the center of the branch using a reverse lark's head knot.

Step 2: Separate the strings into three groups of 10 hanging strings each. Set aside two of the groups to work in one section at a time.

Step 3: Pick up the fifth string from the left and cross it diagonally over the remaining strings on the right. This will serve as the main lead cord for the vine, which the leaves will "stem" from.

Step 4: Tie a row of four diagonal clove hitch knots.

Step 5: Pick up the second string from that row of knots and cross it diagonally toward the left side; this will be the lead cord for the top of the first leaf.

Step 6: Tie a row of four diagonal clove hitch knots with a slight curve to form the top leaf border.

Step 7: Take the sixth string from the left (the top string from the last row of knots) and guide it across all the other strings to the left, in a slightly curved shape. This will form the bottom border of the leaf.

Step 8: Tie a slightly curved row of five diagonal clove hitch knots to form the bottom border of the leaf.

Step 9: Pick up the main vine lead cord from step 4 and redirect it diagonally to the left. Tie a row of seven diagonal clove hitch knots.

Step 10: Count the fifth string from the left and direct it over the remaining four strings to the right in a diagonal line; this will form the top border of the second leaf. Tie a row of four diagonal clove hitch knots in a slightly curved shape.

Step 11: Using the fifth string from the left as the lead cord, tie a row of five diagonal clove hitch knots to form the bottom border.

Step 12: Return to the lead cord from the main vine and redirect it diagonally toward the right. Tie seven diagonal clove hitch knots.

Step 13: Pick up the fifth string from the left and direct it over the other strings on the left. Use the same technique as with the first leaf to create a third leaf in this section.

Step 14: Repeat steps 3 to 13 for the next two groups of 10 hanging strings that were previously set aside. For the center group of strings, tie the main vine with one more length of seven diagonal clove hitch knots after finishing the last leaf.

layer 2

Step 15: Cut six pieces of string into 15-foot (4.6-m) lengths. Divide them into two groups of three strings and attach each group of strings onto the branch approximately 2 inches (5 cm) from the last section using reverse lark's head knots.

Step 16: Take the outer two strings and direct them diagonally inward over the other strings. These will be the main lead strings.

Step 17: Tie a row of diagonal clove hitch knots around the lead strings.

Step 18: Pick up the fourth string from the left and direct it up and to the left, over the other strings.

Step 19: Tie a row of three diagonal clove hitch knots.

Step 20: Redirect the same lead cord back inward.

Step 21: Tie two diagonal clove hitch knots over the next two strings.

Step 22: Take the fourth string from the left and direct it outward, over the other three strings.

Step 23: Tie a row of three diagonal clove hitch knots.

Step 24: Redirect the same lead cord back inward.

Step 25: Tie a row of three diagonal clove hitch knots.

Step 26: Pick up the two main lead cords and direct them diagonally outward, over the remaining strings.

Step 27: Tie a row of four diagonal clove hitch knots around the two main lead cords.

Step 28: Repeat the same pattern four times on this group of strings.

Step 29: Use the same technique on the other group of strings, but mirroring the direction of the knots.

Step 30: Cut one 60-inch (152.4-cm) string. Use it to connect both sections in the center by tying a gathering knot.

layer 3

Step 31: Cut eight strings into 15-foot (4.6-m) lengths. Divide the strings into two groups of four and attach each group to the branch about 2 inches (5 cm) out from the last section using reverse lark's head knots.

Step 32: Pick up the fourth string from the left and cross it inward over the rest of the strings diagonally; this will be one lead cord for the diamond pattern.

Step 33: Tie a row of four diagonal clove hitch knots around the lead cord using the strings to the right.

Step 34: Pick up the fourth string in again, and cross it outward over the rest of the strings diagonally (in the opposite direction from the first row). Tie a row of four diagonal clove hitch knots using the strings to the left. This should create an inverted "V" shape.

Step 35: Setting aside the lead cords, tie a square knot in the center using the two outer working cords.

Step 36: Use the lead cords on each side and direct them both to the center, tying diagonal clove hitch knots into a "V" shape to complete the diamond.

Step 37: Continue tying six diamond patterns on each side, following steps 32 to 36.

Step 38: Join the two sections in the center by using the four center strings from each section to tie a diamond pattern.

Step 39: Continue tying an additional two diagonal clove hitch knots down the left side after the center diamond is complete.

Step 40: Take the top string from the last two diagonal clove hitch knots and direct it to the right to form the top border of the leaf. Refer to the vine technique that was used in layer 1 to create two leaves.

Step 41: Cut 36 strings into 90-inch (228.6-cm) lengths. Attach them with lark's head knots to all the outer strings to form a long fringe. Each section will have three strings attached.

Step 42: Use the third and the fifth groups of strings to create new sections of vines, using the same technique as used in layer 1.

Step 43: Tie two vines on each side of the fringe with two leaves each.

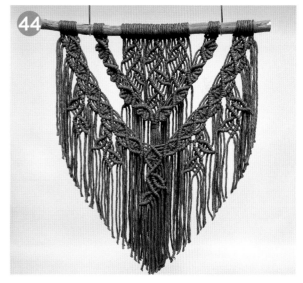

Step 44: Once the vines are finished, trim all ends to the desired length in a "V" shape.

OCEAN

Everyone should have the chance to experience the joy of seeing the ocean at least once in their life. The salty air, the mist from the waves crashing, and the warm sand on your toes—the feeling is almost indescribable. There's no better way to clear out mental clutter than to spend a day walking along the coast, swimming in the water, and soaking in the sunlight. The closest I can get to describing my love for the ocean is to make art inspired by the sights and patterns that emerge when you look a little more closely.

If tidepools were made of string, they'd be filled with some of the adorable projects in this chapter, like the Mermaid Fishtail Keychain (page 113) or pocket-size Macramé Seashell (page 117). Explore some of the shapes found at the beach or under the ocean's surface with projects like the Fish Scale Wall Hanging (page 127) or embrace your inner ocean spirit with the more advanced Ocean Goddess Wall Hanging (page 138).

MERMAID FISHTAIL KEYCHAIN

level: beginner

Take a little piece of the ocean with you everywhere you go with this simple, beginner-friendly macramé keychain. The scale-like design and fishtail trim come together to form a unique and beautiful pattern! You will only need a handful of string and three basic knots to complete this project.

materials

- 3mm teal-colored string: 200 inches (500 cm)
- 1-inch (2.5-cm) keychain clasp
- Measuring tape
- Scissors
- Comb
- Optional: Clipboard

knots used in this project

- Reverse Lark's Head Knot (page 10)
- Diagonal Clove Hitch Knot (page 15)
- Gathering Knot (page 18)

Step 1: Cut four lengths of string to 35 inches (89 cm). Secure the keychain clasp onto the clipboard, if using, then attach the four strings onto the clasp using a reverse lark's head knot.

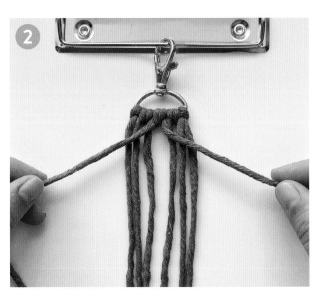

Step 2: Separate the strings in half and grab the two center strings, directing them outward over the remaining three strings on each side. These will serve as the lead cords for the first rows of diagonal clove hitch knots.

Step 3: Tie a row of diagonal clove hitch knots on each side of the keychain at a slight diagonal angle downward, toward the outer edge of the keychain.

Step 4: Once the first row of diagonal clove hitch knots is completed on both sides, take the innermost strings and direct them outward again. These will be the new lead cords for the next row of knots.

Step 5: Tie a second row of diagonal clove hitch knots on each side, just as in step 3 but leaving a bit of space between the new row and the previous row.

Step 6: Once the second row is complete, take the centermost strings and once again direct them outward as new lead strings.

Step 7: For the last row of clove hitch knots, incorporate all previous strings into the next knot so that there are no loose strings. (So after tying the first clove hitch, take the loose string from that knot and bundle it together with the lead cord going forward.)

Step 8: Following the same method as the previous step, tie the last clove hitch knot around all three previous cords to secure all the cords together. Repeat on the other side.

Step 10: Once the gathering knot is complete, use the comb to brush out all of the bottom strings. Be sure to flip the keychain over from front to back to comb it out fully.

Step 9: Once both sides are finished, cut one last section of string to 15 inches (38 cm). Flip the keychain over, gather all the strings together at the bottom, and secure them using a gathering knot.

Step 11: Use fabric scissors and cut at a sharp angle from the outside toward the center to create an inverted "V" shape and give your fish keychain a tail!

MACRAMÉ SEASHELL

level: beginner

If you put your ear to this macramé seashell, you might hear the ocean. Some of my fondest memories as a child were walking along the shoreline in search of the most unique shells I could find. The different colors, sizes, and shapes are endless! This knotted seashell would be adorable styled on a shelf, framed in a shadow box, or even attached as a focal point to a larger wall hanging.

materials

- 5mm dusty blush–colored string: 33.3 feet (10.2 m)
- Measuring tape
- Scissors
- Optional: Superglue or fabric glue

knots used in this project

- Reverse Lark's Head Knot (page 10)
- Diagonal Clove Hitch Knot (page 15)
- Horizontal Clove Hitch Knot (page 16)

Step 1: Cut five pieces of string into 80-inch (203.2-cm) lengths. Take one of the strings and fold it in half, holding at the center loop. This string will become the lead cord through the first half of the seashell pattern.

Step 2: Attach three additional strings to the center loop of the first string using a reverse lark's head knot.

Step 3: Take one end of the lead cord and cross it over the other. Use the string underneath to tie a diagonal clove hitch knot around the string on top.

Step 4: Pull the clove hitch knot tight so that no extra string is showing and the group of knots resembles a somewhat circular shape. Set aside the lead cord from the last clove hitch knot; moving forward through the first half of the seashell pattern, all knots and all new strings will be attached around that lead cord.

Step 5: Attach another string to the lead cord using a reverse lark's head knot. Slide it up on the string until it is snug against the last knot.

Step 6: Tie four horizontal clove hitch knots around the lead cord while rotating to create a circular shape.

Step 7: For the next two strings, tie horizontal clove hitch knots in a straight line pointing away from the center of the circle instead of tightly against the circular shape, as done in the previous few knots.

Step 8: Rotate the piece and pick up the next two strings over from the last clove hitch knots tied in step 7. Use the second string as a lead string and tie a diagonal clove hitch knot over it with the first string.

Step 9: Pick up the next string over from the last two and cross it over both previous strings, leaving a bit of space between this string and the last diagonal clove hitch knot from step 8. This will be the lead cord for a new row of clove hitch knots.

Step 10: Tie two diagonal clove hitch knots over the lead cord.

Step 11: Move down to the next string, crossing it over the previous three strings. Use this string as the lead cord for the next row of clove hitch knots. Tie three diagonal clove hitch knots around the lead cord.

Step 12: Continue in the same method used in steps 8 to 11, using each new string as a lead cord and tying clove hitch knots around it using all previous strings. This will result in a slightly longer row of clove hitch knots each time, creating an expanding look.

Step 13: For the last row of diagonal clove hitch knots, combine the bottom two strings. Use both as lead strings and tie a row of diagonal clove hitch knots around them using all previous strings. There will now be eight loose strings on the bottom, plus the two lead cords coming out of the last row of clove hitch knots.

Step 14: Neatly trim the bottom strings off in the back and trim off the two lead cords, making sure not to cut them so short that the last knots come undone. Optional: If extra security is desired to keep the trimmed strings from coming loose, a few dabs of superglue or fabric glue can be applied to the loose ends in the back.

RIPTIDE WOVEN HOOP

level: beginner

The ocean can be paradoxically serene and wild. It is untamable and beautiful. A riptide is a stretch of turbulent water that is caused by the meeting of two different currents. It is commonly known for pulling swimmers in toward the deeper water and is so strong that it is difficult to swim against. Let's admire the turbulence of the ocean from the comfort and safety of dry land while creating this riptide hoop pattern.

materials

- 3mm string:
  - White: 63.3 feet (19.3 m)
  - Peacock blue: 33.3 feet (10.2 m)
- 10-inch (25.4-cm) metal hoop
- Measuring tape
- Scissors
- Comb

knots used in this project

- Horizontal Clove Hitch Knot (page 16)

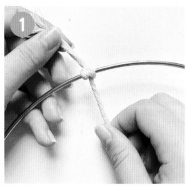

Step 1: Cut 38 pieces of white string into 20-inch (50.8-cm) lengths. Attach all 38 strings to the hoop using horizontal clove hitch knots, making sure to leave about 2 inches (5 cm) of string loose on the outside of the hoop.

Step 2: Once each of the white strings is attached, push them all tightly together and position them at the top of the hoop.

Step 3: Cut 20 pieces of blue string into 20-inch (50.8-cm) lengths. Attach all 20 strings on the left-hand side of the hoop using horizontal clove hitch knots. Leave about 2 inches (5 cm) of string loose on the outside of the hoop.

Step 4: Tighten the blue strings and make sure they are all pressed tightly against each other.

Step 5: Place the longer ends of the blue strings toward the right side of the hoop, and the longer ends of the white strings toward the bottom of the hoop. Make sure the white strings all sit on top of the blue strings.

Step 6: Secure all of the white strings to the bottom of the hoop using horizontal clove hitch knots, making sure all the strings are pulled tightly.

Step 7: Take the lowest seven blue strings and cross them up and over the white strings. Tie them tightly to the right side of the hoop using horizontal clove hitch knots.

NOTE: The next 10 strings will be used to create the "wave" shape. They will be labeled from 1 to 10, moving from the bottom to the top.

Step 8: Cross string #1 over the first three white strings, under the next three, and then back to the top.

Step 9: Cross string #2 under the first eight strings and then back to the top.

Cross string #3 under the first 10 strings and then back to the top.

Cross string #4 under the first 12 strings and then back to the top.

Continue this pattern, adding increments of two white strings for each row of blue strings to go under, until you have finished all 10 blue strings.

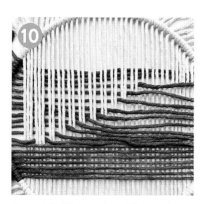

Step 10: There should now be three remaining blue strings above string #10. Leave them underneath the white strings.

Step 11: Cross string #10 on top of only one white string, then feed it back under the remaining white strings and over to the other side of the hoop.

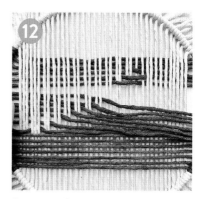

Step 12: Cross string #9 over four white strings, then feed it back under the remaining strings. Cross string #8 over five white strings and then back under the rest.

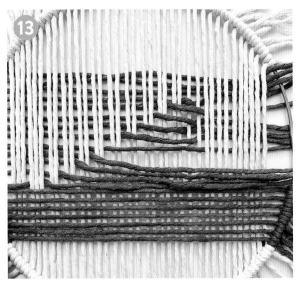

Step 13: Cross string #7 over six white strings, then back under.

Cross string #6 over nine white strings, then back under.

Cross string #5 over 12 white strings, then back under.

Step 14: Cross string #4 over 15 white strings, then back under.

Cross string #3 over 19 white strings, then back under.

Cross string #2 over 23 white strings, then back under.

Cross string #1 over 27 white strings, then back under.

Step 15: Once all strings are woven through, tightly secure all of the blue strings to the right side of the hoop using horizontal clove hitch knots.

Step 16: Use a comb to brush out the outer strings of the hoop into fringe.

Step 17: Trim the fringe, following along the curve of the hoop to create a rounded shape.

FISH SCALE WALL HANGING

level: beginner/intermediate

I've always loved the interesting shapes that can be found in nature. Patterns can emerge from anywhere when you look for them! This wall hanging captures the beautiful scalloped shapes of fish scales in a subtle way for a structured, modern-looking macramé piece.

While the concept and design of this piece is very simple, some of the clove hitch knots may be slightly more challenging. This should be a fairly beginner-friendly piece, but make sure you're familiar with the clove hitch knot and practice tying diagonal clove hitch knots from multiple angles and directions first.

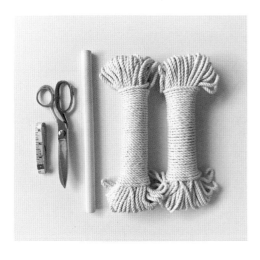

materials

- 5mm natural rope: 200 feet (61 m)
- 12-inch (30.5-cm) dowel
- Measuring tape
- Scissors
- Comb
- Optional: S-hooks and working rack

knots used in this project

- Reverse Lark's Head Knot (page 10)
- Diagonal Clove Hitch Knot (page 15)
- Horizontal Clove Hitch Knot (page 16)

Step 1: Cut 20 pieces of rope to 120 inches (304.8 cm). Attach all 20 pieces to the dowel using a reverse lark's head knot.

Step 2: Separate the rope into four sections of 10 hanging lengths. Each section will be made into one "scale" in the first row.

Step 3: Each section's ropes will be referenced in numbers from 1 to 10, with #1 being the rope farthest to the left and #10 being the rope farthest to the right. Pick up rope #1 (left side) and cross it over the other cords diagonally (at a 45-degree angle) toward the center. This will act as a lead cord for a row of diagonal clove hitch knots.

Step 4: Use ropes #2, #3, and #4 to tie a row of diagonal clove hitch knots around the lead cord.

Step 5: Pick up rope #10 and cross it over the other ropes diagonally (at a 45-degree angle) toward the center. This will act as the lead cord for another row of diagonal clove hitch knots.

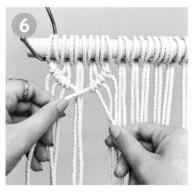

Step 6: Use ropes #9, #8, and #7 to tie a row of diagonal clove hitch knots around the lead cord.

Step 7: Cross the two lead cords over each other and pinch them together in the center. The last two horizontal clove hitch knots, using ropes #5 and #6, will each be tied around both lead cords.

Step 8: For ropes #5 and #6, tie horizontal clove hitch knots. Make sure that each clove hitch knot is tied around both lead cords.

Step 9: There will likely be some extra space where the two lead cords are showing through the last two knots. Gently pull on the lead cords on the bottom to tighten up the row and make it look more uniform. You may need to tug at some of the rope or knots a bit until everything looks even.

Step 10: Repeat steps 3 to 9 in the next three groups of rope until you have created the first row of four scales.

Step 11: Count five strings in on both the left and right sides of the wall hanging. Pick up those ropes and point them diagonally toward the outer edges of the wall hanging.

Step 12: Use those two ropes as lead cords and tie a new row of diagonal clove hitch knots on each side. Try to tie them with a slight curve upward at the end.

Step 13: Moving through the rest of the row, the center two cords from each previous scale will be used as the new lead cords for the scales. For example, rope #6 from the first scale and rope #5 from the second scale will be used as lead cords, joining in the center to create a new scale.

Step 14: Continue using the same technique as in the first row of scales (steps 3 to 10) to create a new row.

Step 15: Continue adding new rows of scales, each time remembering to use the center ropes from each previous row as the lead cords for a new scale.

Step 16: Complete seven rows of scales in total.

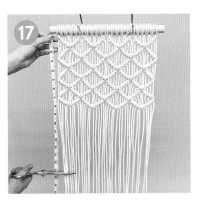

Step 17: Trim the bottom to the desired length; my preference is 16 inches (40.6 cm).

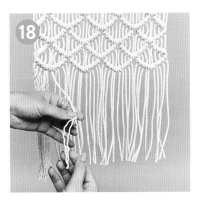

Step 18: Untwist the hanging rope at the bottom to create a fuller fringe, starting at the bottom and working upward. If needed, give one final trim to even out all of the bottom fringe.

THALIA BEACH LANDSCAPE

level: intermediate

Thalia Street Beach is one of the most beautiful beaches in Laguna Beach, California. It is well known for its gentle and consistent wave break, making it a great spot to learn how to surf. Aside from surfing, it is just a magical place to sit and relax. The sun glitters on the water as the tide ebbs and flows, and the warm sand coaxes you to simply lie down and look out over the ocean. This Thalia wall hanging is my attempt to capture the warm glow of blissful days spent enjoying the ocean. The challenge here is in keeping even tension and tying the knots to perfection so the design comes through looking smooth, not chunky or pixelated.

materials

- 5mm string:
  - White: 195 feet (59.4 m)
  - Teal: 135 feet (41.1 m)
  - Yellow/mustard: 16.7 feet (5.1 m)
  - Peacock blue: 66.7 feet (20.3 m)
- 17-inch (43.2-cm) branch or dowel
- Measuring tape
- Scissors
- Large tapestry needle
- Comb
- Optional: S-hooks and working rack

knots used in this project

- Reverse Lark's Head Knot (page 10)
- Alternating Colors Square Knot Method (page 21)
- Square Knot (page 13)

Step 1: Cut 28 white strings into 55-inch (139.7-cm) lengths. Attach all strings to the branch or dowel using reverse lark's head knots; each section of four hanging strings will be referred to as one "column," numbered 1 to 14 from left to right.

Step 2: Cut four teal strings into 180-inch (457.2-cm) lengths. Attach the four strings to columns 1, 2, 13, and 14 using the alternating colors square knot method.

Step 3: Tie continuous teal square knots down columns 1, 2, 13, and 14 according to the lengths in the diagram on page 137.

Step 4: Cut 10 more teal strings to 60-inch (152.4-cm) lengths and attach to columns 3 to 12 using the alternating colors square knot method.

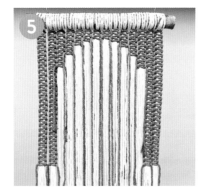

Step 5: Tie continuous square knots using the teal string down columns 3 to 12 according to the lengths in the diagram.

Step 6: Cut 10 white strings to 80-inch (203.2-cm) lengths. Attach to columns 3 to 12 using the alternating colors square knot method, then trim off the teal working cords from the previous section in the back.

Step 7: Tie continuous square knots using the white string in columns 3 to 12 according to the lengths in the diagram.

Step 8: Cut four yellow strings to 50-inch (127-cm) lengths for the sun section. Attach them to columns 5 to 8 using the alternating colors square knot method.

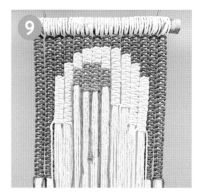

Step 9: Tie continuous square knots with the yellow string over all six hanging strings (including the working cords from the previous white section). Tie continuous square knots according to the lengths in the diagram.

Step 10: Once the sun section is complete, alternate back to the white working cord in columns 5 to 8 by bringing the two white strings forward while pushing the yellow cords back.

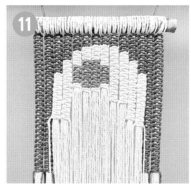

Step 11: Once a white square knot has been tied in columns 5 to 8, trim off the ends of the yellow strings in the back.

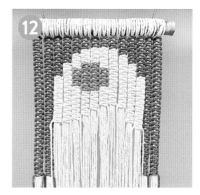

Step 12: Continue tying white square knots in columns 5 to 8 according to the lengths in the diagram.

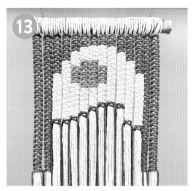

Step 13: Cut 10 blue strings into 80-inch (203.2-cm) lengths for the wave section. Attach to columns 3 to 12 using the alternating colors square knot method.

Step 14: For column 10, attach one blue square knot, then alternate back to the white strings. Tie 1½ white square knots, then switch back to blue.

Step 15: Tie continuous square knots down columns 3 to 12 using the blue strings according to the lengths in the diagram. All blue columns should form an even line across the bottom. If any columns are uneven, add or remove knots as needed.

Step 16: Cut 10 more teal strings into 30-inch (76.2-cm) lengths. Attach to columns 3 to 12 using the alternating colors square knot method.

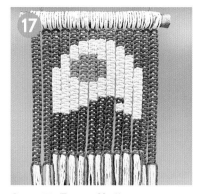

Step 17: Trim off all previous working cords in the back.

Step 18: Tie continuous teal square knots according to the lengths in the diagram. Once all sections are finished, make sure the bottoms all end in a straight line. If any sections need adjustment, add or remove knots until the bottom is even.

Step 19: Flip the piece over to the back. Use a tapestry needle to weave in the loose strings on the bottom upward through the last square knot in the back. Trim off the loose ends once they are secured.

1	2	3	4	5	6	7	8	9	10	11	12	13	14
						1" (2.5 cm)	1" (2.5 cm)						
			3" (7.6 cm)	2" (5 cm)	1.5" (3.8 cm)			1.5" (3.8 cm)	2" (5 cm)	3" (7.6 cm)			
				1.5" (3.8 cm)	1.5" (3.8 cm)	2" (5 cm)	2.5" (6.4 cm)						
		4.5" (11.4 cm)		1.5" (3.8 cm)	2.5" (6.4 cm)	2.5" (6.4 cm)	1.5" (3.8 cm)				4.5" (11.4 cm)		
							2.5" (6.4 cm)	6" (15.2 cm)	5.5" (14 cm)				
									0.5" (1.3 cm)				
						2.5" (6.4 cm)							
					3.5" (8.9 cm)								
				4" (10.2 cm)					1" (2.5 cm)				
			6.5" (16.5 cm)								6.5" (16.5 cm)		
		5" (12.7 cm)											
											6" (15.2 cm)		
		4" (10.2 cm)	4" (10.2 cm)	4.5" (11.4 cm)	5" (12.7 cm)	5.5" (14 cm)	6" (15.2 cm)	6.5" (16.5 cm)	5" (12.7 cm)	4.5" (11.4 cm)	4" (10.2 cm)		
15" (38.1 cm)	15" (38.1 cm)	1.5" (3.8 cm)	1.5" (3.8 cm)	1.5" (3.8 cm)	1.5" (3.8 cm)	1.5" (3.8 cm)	1.5" (3.8 cm)	1.5" (3.8 cm)	1.5" (3.8 cm)	1.5" (3.8 cm)	1.5" (3.8 cm)	15" (38.1 cm)	15" (38.1 cm)

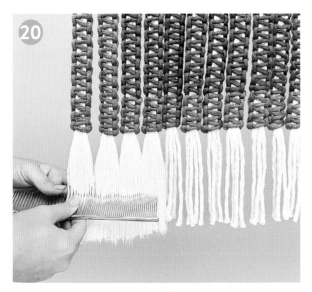

Step 20: Cut the bottom of the hanging strings to the desired length and use the comb to brush the strings out into fringe. Trim once more, if needed, to even out the ends.

OCEAN GODDESS WALL HANGING

level: advanced

A closer look at this multilayered wall hanging will reveal three different ocean-inspired patterns within: a shell and two different wave designs. This piece is ornate and ethereal and would work well made in a variety of different beachy colors.

This wall hanging builds upon some of the beginner ocean-themed projects, like the fishtail keychain pattern, but expands upon them and introduces some more complicated layers and clove hitch knot designs.

materials

- 5mm teal string: 520 feet (158.5 m)
- 22-inch (56-cm) branch or dowel
- Measuring tape
- Scissors
- Optional: S-hooks and working rack

knots used in this project

- Reverse Lark's Head Knot (page 10)
- Diagonal Clove Hitch Knot (page 15)
- Square Knot (page 13)

layer 1

Step 1: Cut 10 pieces of string into 8-foot (2.4-m) lengths. Attach all 10 strings to the center of the branch using a reverse lark's head knot.

Step 2: Separate the strings in half and grab the two center strings, directing each diagonally outward on each side over the other strings. These will serve as lead cords for the first rows of diagonal clove hitch knots.

Step 3: Tie a row of diagonal clove hitch knots on each side at a slight diagonal angle downward, toward the outer edge.

Step 4: Once the first row of diagonal clove hitch knots is completed on both sides, take the innermost strings and direct them outward again. These will be the new lead cords for the next row of knots.

Step 5: Tie a second row of diagonal clove hitch knots on each side, just as in step 4 but leaving a bit of space between the new row and the previous row.

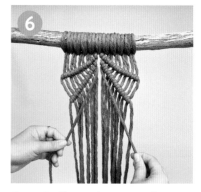

Step 6: Once the second row is complete, take the centermost strings and once again direct them outward as the new lead strings. Leave similar spacing as in the last two rows, so the lead cords will almost be pointing directly downward.

Step 7: Tie a third row of diagonal clove hitch knots on each side.

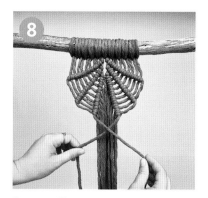

Step 8: Take the lead cords from the last row and cross them both toward the center.

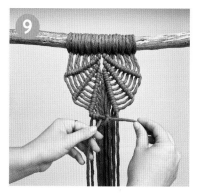

Step 9: Tie two diagonal clove hitch knots on each side using the next two strings over from the lead cord.

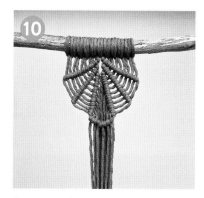

Step 10: Connect the two lead strings in the center using one to tie a clove hitch knot over the other.

Step 11: Cut 18 pieces of string into 50-inch (127-cm) lengths. Divide the strings into groups of three, attaching each group to one of the outer strings of the shell pattern using a reverse lark's head knot.

layer 2

Step 12: Cut eight pieces of string into 10-foot (3-m) lengths. Separate them into two groups of four strings each, and use reverse lark's head knots to attach each group approximately 2 inches (5 cm) outward from layer 1.

Step 13: Tie two square knots at the top, as close to the branch as possible.

Step 14: Using the two innermost strings from the top two square knots, create another square knot directly underneath with little to no space between knots.

Step 15: Repeat steps 13 and 14, creating alternating rows of square knots, tying 20 rows total on one side.

Step 16: Repeat steps 13 and 14 on the group of strings on the other side of the wall hanging, continuing until you have tied 20 rows total.

Step 17: Join the two sections together in the center, and use the two inner strings from each side to tie a square knot.

Step 18: Tie a row of alternating square knots directly under the center square knot using two additional strings from either side.

Step 19: Tie one more square knot underneath using the four center strings.

Step 20: Cut 18 pieces of string into 50-inch (127-cm) lengths. Attach one string to each segment of space on the outer edge of this layer using reverse lark's head knots.

layer 3

Step 21: Cut eight pieces of string into 17-foot (5.2-m) lengths. Divide the strings into two sections of four strings each, and attach each group of strings to the branch approximately 2 inches (5 cm) apart from the layer 2 section using a reverse lark's head knot.

Step 22: Take the third string (counting from the outside in) and direct it diagonally inward over the remaining strings.

Step 23: Use that string as a lead cord and tie a row of diagonal clove hitch knots using the rest of the strings it is crossing over.

Step 24: Take the second string and direct it underneath the last row.

Step 25: Use this string to form a new row of diagonal clove hitch knots, leaving the last string out from the row.

Step 26: Take the outermost string and move it in the same direction as the last two rows. This will be the new lead cord.

Step 27: Use the string to form one more row of diagonal clove hitch knots, leaving the last two strings out from the row.

Step 28: Take the same lead cord from the last step and this time direct it the opposite way, back toward the outer edge but still at a diagonal angle.

Step 29: Tie a row of diagonal clove hitch knots around the lead cord using all remaining strings.

Step 30: Take the second lead cord from the inside and direct it outward, under the last row. Tie a row of diagonal clove hitch knots, again leaving out the last string.

Step 31: Take the last lead cord and direct it to the outer edge as well. Tie one more row of clove hitch knots around this lead cord, leaving out the last two strings.

Step 32: Repeat steps 22 to 31 three more times to create a total of four soft "wave" shapes.

Step 33: Use the same technique from steps 22 to 31 on the group of strings on the other side of the wall hanging, but mirror the direction of the waves. Bring both sections together in the center.

Step 34: Take the two innermost strings from each side and bring them together, crossing one over the other. Tie a clove hitch knot to connect them.

Step 35: Use those two strings as lead cords to tie two diagonal rows of clove hitch knots, forming an inverted "V" shape with a total of six knots on each side.

Step 36: Take the lead cord from the left side and direct it inward. This will serve as the first lead cord to create the wave shape in the center.

Step 37: Point the lead cord slightly upward, toward the top of the inverted "V." Tie diagonal clove hitch knots using the first five strings.

Step 38: Change the direction of the lead cord to point slightly more downward for two more diagonal clove hitch knots.

Step 39: Pick up the working cord from the last clove hitch knot that was tied. This will be the lead cord for the rest of the wave.

Step 40: Use the working cord directly to the left of the new lead cord to tie one clove hitch knot.

Step 41: Redirect the same lead cord to the right.

Step 42: Use all remaining strings to the right to tie a row of diagonal clove hitch knots, pointing to the right corner of the inverted "V" shape.

Step 43: Take the outermost cords of the inverted "V" and use them as lead cords to create a regular "V"-shaped row of diagonal clove hitch knots downward and back toward the center.

Step 44: Where both lead cords meet, tie one clove hitch knot to complete the diamond shape.

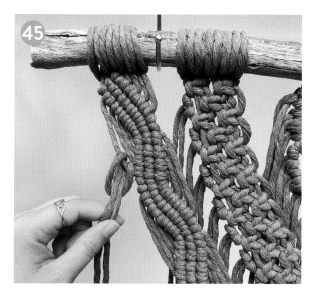

Step 45: Cut 40 pieces of string into 22-inch (56-cm) lengths. Separate the strings into eight groups of five strings each, then use reverse lark's head knots to add each group to an outer edge on this layer.

Step 46: Trim all excess string at the bottom to a rounded "V" shape until both sides are even and trimmed to the desired length.

EARTH AND SKY

I am forever inspired by the textures, sights, and experiences in nature. There are so many natural elements that don't fit into a tidy category, but are just as worthy of being celebrated. From vast entities like the sun and moon to small intricacies like the feather of a bird, inspiration can come from anywhere. Some of these projects are meant to motivate you to get right out and explore, while others are created to help you appreciate nature from afar.

I'm excited to introduce some more functional patterns in this section to help you connect with nature in a more hands-on way. The Bird Nesting Bag (page 155) is something that both you and our winged friends can enjoy, and the Foraging Pouch (page 173) is the perfect place to store edible mushrooms or other treasures found in the woods. The Sun Mandala (page 161) and the Luna Wall Hanging (page 165) remind us of the vast beauty of those far away, celestial bodies.

MACRAMÉ FEATHER

level: beginner

The macramé feather is fluffy, textured, and so beautifully simple—no wonder this trend, which was originally started by macramé artist Kari Oakes, took the macramé world by storm! This version of the macramé feather is created by using a similar technique as my macramé landscapes: by attaching one string to another set of strings using a version of the square knot. Hang it on the wall or attach it to another project to experience its full beauty!

materials

- 5mm string:
  - Accent color (I used mocha): 6.5 feet (2 m)
  - White: 25.3 feet (7.7 m)
- 1 large bead
- Measuring tape
- Scissors
- Comb

knots used in this project

- Alternating Colors Square Knot Method (page 21)

Step 1: Cut one piece of the accent color string to 30 inches (76.2 cm) long. Fold it in half to create a loop at the top; these will be the lead cords around which all other strings will be attached.

Step 2: Slide the bead over the loop. If the bead is loose and may fall off too easily, tie a simple overhand knot right above the bead on the loop.

Step 3: Cut 19 pieces of white string and three pieces of the accent color string (21 pieces total) to 16-inch (40.6-cm) lengths. Take a white string and place the center of it behind the lead cords.

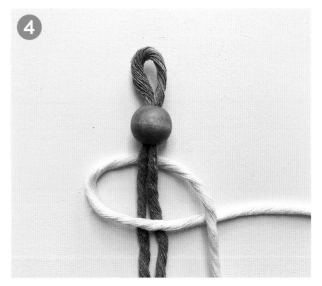

Step 4: Bring the left side over to the right, crossing it on top of the lead cords and then underneath the cord on the right.

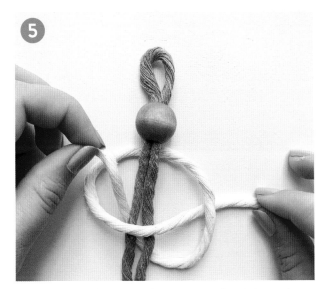

Step 5: Take the string that was on the right and bring it to the left, crossing it under the lead cords and then bringing it up through the loop. Then pull the outer ends to tighten.

Step 6: Repeat steps 4 and 5 but in reverse; take the right string and bring it to the left, going over the lead cords and then under the left string.

Step 7: Take the left string and pull it to the right, behind the lead cords and through the loop on the right.

Step 8: Pull on the two ends to tighten. Then, use your thumb to gently slide the whole knot upward until it sits snugly below the bead. You have just completed the alternating colors square knot method to attach the first string!

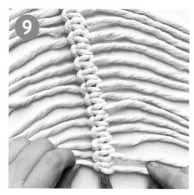

Step 9: Continue using the alternating colors square knot method to attach the first 18 white strings.

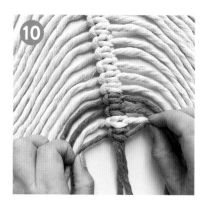

Step 10: Use the same alternating colors square knot method to attach two accent color strings, the last white string, and finally one more accent string.

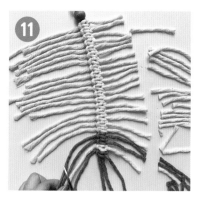

Step 11: Trim all strings to just over 2 inches (5 cm) in length, leaving the bottom few strings a bit longer.

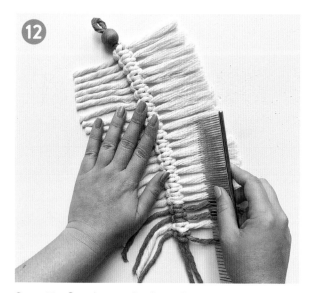

Step 12: Comb out all of the fringe, flipping the feather from front to back to make sure the fringe is combed out fully and evenly.

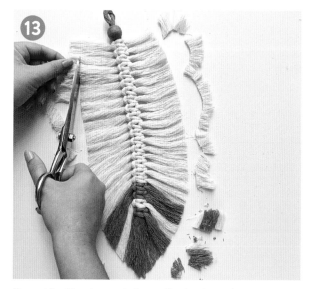

Step 13: Go through for a final trim, cleaning up all edges and refining the feather shape.

TIP: Spray the feather with fabric stiffener or hairspray if you'd like it to hold its shape more perfectly when hanging on the wall.

BIRD NESTING BAG

level: beginner

Springtime is bird nesting season and when that time comes, birds are busy gathering and sorting through materials they can use. While they are experts at building their own nests, this project can be a great way to help make their task easier and a great bird-watching activity for you. When filling your bag, opt for organic materials. Some great nest-building materials include dead leaves, dried grass clippings, very small cotton string or twine scraps (nothing long enough that a bird could get tangled in), and twigs or pine needles. Avoid using things like plastic or dryer lint, as these can be harmful to the bird and their nest.

materials

- 5mm natural string: 84.6 feet (25.8 m)
- Measuring tape
- Scissors
- Scraps to fill bag with
- Optional: S-hooks and working rack or tape to anchor project to a surface

knots used in this project

- Lark's Head Knot (page 10)
- Single Strand Lark's Head Knot (page 11)
- Reverse Lark's Head Knot (page 10)
- Square Knot (page 13)
- Gathering Knot (page 18)

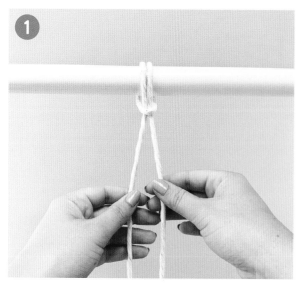

Step 1: Cut 15 strings into 65-inch (165.1-cm) lengths. Attach one string directly to the top of the working rack using a lark's head knot (or tape one end down to your work surface if working horizontally). The loose string on the left side should be 25 inches (64 cm) long, with all remaining length hanging on the right.

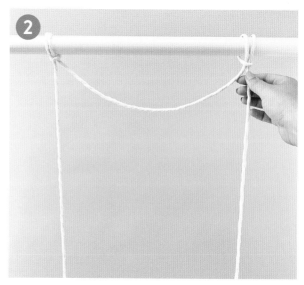

Step 2: Pick up the longer side on the right, and attach it to the rack approximately 12 inches (30.5 cm) to the right of the first knot using a single strand lark's head knot. Allow some slack in the string between the two knots so that it is hanging loosely.

Step 3: Attach the remaining 14 strings to the draped segment of string using reverse lark's head knots.

Step 4: Once all 14 strings are attached, use groups of four hanging strings at a time to tie a horizontal row of square knots. This will result in a total of seven square knots.

Step 5: Allowing approximately 1 inch (2.5 cm) of space below the first row, tie a row of alternating square knots. This means that each square knot in this row will be comprised of two strings from each of the previous square knots in the row above. The second row of knots will contain only six square knots, with two unused strings on each side.

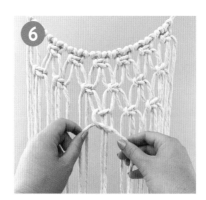

Step 6: Tie another row of alternating square knots another 1 inch (2.5 cm) below the last row. The third row will contain only five knots, leaving four strings hanging unused on each side. Note that a "V" shape is beginning to form in the pattern.

Step 7: Continue making rows of alternating square knots 1 inch (2.5 cm) below the last row until there are six rows of square knots total. The sixth row should only contain two square knots.

Step 8: Gently push the two lark's head knots that are attaching the project to the working rack together.

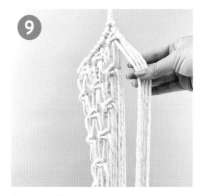

Step 9: Find the two top untied strings from both sides, and join them together using a square knot. This knot should be aligned with the second row of square knots.

Step 10: For the next row, split the strings from the previous square knot in half. Join each set of two strings with two strings on either side. Tie two square knots, aligning both knots with the third row.

Step 11: Continue to tie alternating square knots with all loose strings until you have completely closed the "seam." The project should look like a loosely netted tube with six rows of square knots going evenly all the way around.

Step 12: Cut one additional piece of string to 40 inches (101.6 cm) long. Bundle all the strings together on the bottom and secure them using a gathering knot.

Step 13: Trim the top string from the gathering knot.

Step 14: Trim the strings at the bottom to approximately 3 inches (7.6 cm) in length.

Step 15: From the opening at the top, fill the loosely netted bag with bird nest–friendly items such as shredded paper, natural fibers, and more.

Step 16: Cinch the opening of the bag closed by pushing all the strings together at the top. This will keep the contents of the bag from easily spilling out. Remove it from the working rack and use the top two strings to tie the bag to a tree branch outside so the birds can enjoy it!

SUN MANDALA

level: beginner/intermediate

The sun has often been used as a symbol of life, energy, clarity, and more. It's difficult to deny the impact that the sun has on us and our well-being, so it's no wonder that many ancient cultures worshipped the sun in some form. This sun mandala has an earthy, bohemian look and can be styled in a variety of ways. While this project is repetitive and mostly beginner-friendly, the switching sides of the horizontal clove hitch knot does create an added challenge.

materials

- 5mm yellow/mustard string: 266.7 feet (81.3 m)
- 10-inch (25.4-cm) metal hoop
- Measuring tape
- Scissors
- Comb

knots used in this project

- Reverse Lark's Head Knot (page 10)
- Horizontal Clove Hitch Knot (page 16)
- Gathering Knot (page 18)

Step 1: Cut 32 pieces of string into 60-inch (152.4-cm) lengths. Attach four pieces at the bottom of the hoop using a reverse lark's head knot.

Step 2: Pick up the string on the left and cross it horizontally to the right, over the other seven strings. This will act as the lead cord for all clove hitch knots in this section.

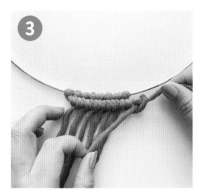

Step 3: Tie a single row of horizontal clove hitch knots, moving from left to right.

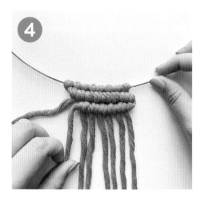

Step 4: Take the same lead cord and redirect it toward the left side. Tie another row of six horizontal clove hitch knots (leaving out the seventh string), this time moving from right to left.

Step 5: Cross the same lead cord back over to the right and tie another row of five horizontal clove hitch knots from left to right. Leave out the last string from the new row as you did with the previous step.

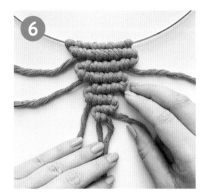

Step 6: Continue this pattern until you have completed four more rows, each time redirecting the lead cord toward the opposite side and leaving out the last cord from each row of knots. The final row should have only one clove hitch knot.

Step 7: Gather all the loose strings together at the bottom.

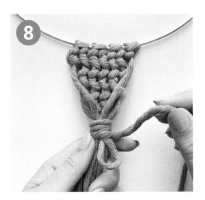

Step 8: Cut 16 pieces of string into 20-inch (50.8-cm) lengths to be used for gathering knots. Flip the hoop around to the back and tie a gathering knot (wrapping the string around three or four times) to secure all loose cords.

Step 9: Gently tug the strings underneath the gathering knot to make sure none of them are loose. Then, cut the string on the top of the gathering knot.

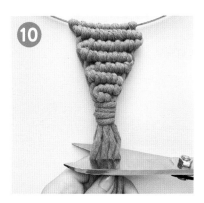

Step 10: Flip the hoop back to the front and trim the bottom strings to just over 1 inch (2.5 cm) in length.

Step 11: Gently brush out the fringe with a comb, making sure not to snag it on any knots.

Step 12: Trim one more time so that all the fringe is even.

Step 13: Cut 24 sections of string to 40-inch (101.6-cm) lengths. For the next section, add three of these strings to the hoop using a reverse lark's head knot.

Step 14: Take the string on the left and cross it over to the right horizontally to form the lead string.

Step 15: Tie a full row of horizontal clove hitch knots, moving from left to right. Continue on as with the previous section in steps 2 to 6, reversing the direction of the lead cord after each row and then skipping the last cord of each row until you have reached a final row of only one horizontal clove hitch knot.

Step 16: Flip the hoop over to the back and once again tie a gathering knot with one of the 20-inch (50.8-cm) strings.

Step 17: Trim off the top string from the gathering knot. Trim the end strings to approximately 1 inch (2.5 cm) and use the comb to brush out the fringe. Give the strings one final trim after combing.

Step 18: Continue alternating between sections with four strings and sections with three strings. There should be eight sections of each size when finished, or 16 sections total.

LUNA WALL HANGING

level: intermediate

The moon is powerful. It controls the tides and, as some would argue, even our moods and energy. It's hard not to be fascinated with the serene beauty of the moon, especially when a full moon lights up the dark night or a slim crescent moon delicately hangs in the sky. This wall hanging uses vertical clove hitch knots to depict a crescent moon with some stars shining around it. This is an alternative technique to my signature alternating colors square knot method, and another way of creating a flat image out of knots. The use of tightly knotted, intricate vertical knots with a nonlinear design may prove to be a challenge, making this piece a more intermediate-level wall hanging even with its small size.

materials

- 5mm string:
  - White: 100.8 feet (30.7 m)
  - Yellow/mustard: 24.8 feet (7.5 m)
- 8-inch (20.3-cm) branch or dowel
- Measuring tape
- Scissors
- Tapestry needle
- Optional: S-hooks and working rack

knots used in this project

- Reverse Lark's Head Knot (page 10)
- Vertical Clove Hitch Knot (page 17)

Step 1: Cut 14 white strings to 35-inch (89-cm) lengths. Attach all 14 strings to the branch or dowel using a reverse lark's head knot.

Step 2: Cut 12 more white strings to 5-foot (1.5-m) lengths. Leaving about 4 inches (10 cm) of string loose on the left-hand side, use one of the strings just cut to tie vertical clove hitch knots across the top. Move from left to right, tying one knot over every two hanging strings.

Step 3: Continue tying vertical clove hitch knots until the entire row has been completed.

Step 4: Take another white string and tie a second row of vertical clove hitch knots, stopping at the third to last pair of hanging strings.

Step 5: Cut a yellow string to 15 inches (38.1 cm) long and tie one yellow vertical clove hitch knot around the next pair of strings.

Step 6: Pushing the loose yellow strings to the back, grab the loose end of the white working cord from this row and carry it over in the back to the next pair of hanging strings. Finish the row with two more white vertical clove hitch knots.

Step 7: For row 3, tie five full vertical clove hitch knots, and on the sixth pair of hanging strings, tie only the first *half* of a vertical clove hitch knot.

Step 8: Cut seven yellow strings to 36-inch (91.4-cm) lengths for the moon section. Attach one yellow string directly under the half clove hitch knot on the sixth pair of strings, tying another half vertical clove hitch.

Step 9: Continue tying three more full yellow vertical clove hitch knots, then carry the white working cord over in the back and tie one more half of a vertical clove hitch.

Step 10: Tie a final yellow vertical half clove hitch directly under the white vertical half clove hitch, then push the yellow working cord to the back.

Step 11: Continue the rest of row 3 with white vertical clove hitch knots.

Step 12: For the fourth row, begin by tying four vertical white clove hitch knots, followed by four vertical yellow clove hitch knots, then four more white vertical clove hitch knots.

Step 13: Cut another yellow string to 15 inches (38.1 cm) long and tie one vertical clove hitch knot on the second to last pair of hanging strings, then switch back to white for the last knot.

Step 14: For the next four rows (rows 5 to 8) tie three white vertical clove hitches first, followed by four vertical yellow clove hitches and then the last seven vertical clove hitches in white.

Step 15: The ninth row will start with four white vertical clove hitches, then four yellow vertical clove hitches, then six white vertical clove hitches.

Step 16: For the tenth row, start by tying five full white vertical clove hitch knots. For the sixth pair of hanging strings, tie half of a yellow vertical clove hitch knot, followed by three full vertical yellow clove hitch knots. Then tie one more yellow half of a vertical clove hitch over the tenth pair of hanging strings.

Step 17: In the same row, pick up the white working cord again and tie one half of a vertical clove hitch under the first yellow half clove hitch.

Step 18: Bring the white cord to the back and carry it over to the next yellow half of a vertical clove hitch knot. Tie another half vertical clove hitch knot underneath that using the white cord, then complete the row using the white string.

Step 19: Cut another 15-inch (38.1-cm) length of yellow string and tie a row of white vertical clove hitch knots, with only one yellow vertical clove hitch knot around the third pair of strings.

Step 20: For the last row, use only the white cord to tie vertical clove hitch knots.

Step 21: Trim all the working cords hanging from the sides into 4-inch (10-cm) lengths.

Step 22: Flip the piece around to clean up all the loose ends in the back. Trim any hanging strings in the back to 4-inch (10-cm) lengths.

Step 23: For all of the hanging yellow strings in the back, use one of two options to secure the loose ends before trimming:

Option A: Knot two nearby yellow strings together using a simple overhand knot, then trim the ends. This option is a bit easier, but will result in a messier look than option B.

Option B: Feed the loose ends through the eye of the tapestry needle, then pull the needle through a knot in the back to tightly weave the ends in, then trim the loose ends. This is my preferred option.

Step 24: Feed the ends of the white strings through the tapestry needle, then push the needle through a knot in the back of the wall hanging. Gently pull the needle and then the string though.

Step 25: Repeat step 24 until all ends are secured.

Step 26: Trim off all loose ends.

Step 27: Once all of the loose strings are tucked and trimmed, trim the hanging strings to the desired length.

FORAGING POUCH

level: intermediate

The pastime of foraging has made a huge resurgence, with people all over the globe looking to reconnect with nature by responsibly gathering various specimens from the woods and forest. Foraging is an art form itself, with so much skill and knowledge needed to understand which discoveries are treasure and which can be dangerous. This bag is the perfect little gathering pouch for whatever you're foraging for, whether it be unique geodes or tasty, edible fungi. We will use mostly square knots in this project, but will learn some new methods that can be translated into other functional items or handbags.

materials

- 5mm string:
  - Main color (I used mocha): 310 feet (94.5 m)
  - Accent color (I used white): 30 inches (76.2 cm)
- Measuring tape
- Scissors
- 2 large beads
- 2 x 1-inch (5 x 2.5-cm) swivel clasps

knots used in this project

- Reverse Lark's Head Knot (page 10)
- Square Knot (page 13)
- Diagonal Clove Hitch Knot (page 15)
- Gathering Knot (page 18)

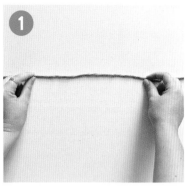

Step 1: Cut 30 main color strings into 9-foot (2.7-m) lengths. Take one of those 30 strings and lay it horizontally across the work surface. This will be considered the lead string for the other strings to attach to.

Step 2: Use a reverse lark's head knot to attach each of the remaining 29 strings to the center portion of the horizontal string.

Step 3: Once all 29 strings are attached, use four hanging strings at a time to tie square knots across the top.

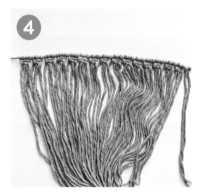

Step 4: After the first row is complete, there will be 15 full square knots and two additional hanging strings at the end. Leave those last two strings for a later step.

Step 5: Fold the entire set of strings in half, joining the two lead strings together.

Step 6: Take one of the lead strings and tie a diagonal clove hitch knot around the other. It does not matter which of the two lead strings you use to tie the knot.

Step 7: Combine the two lead strings with the two leftover strings from step 4.

Step 8: Use these four strings to tie a square knot.

Step 9: Tie alternating square knots directly below the first row of knots. This means that each square knot in this row will be composed of two strings from each of the previous square knots in the row above.

Step 10: Continue tying alternating square knots until the second row is complete.

Step 11: Tie a third row of alternating square knots directly below the last row, this time tying two consecutive square knots instead of one. This is where the drawstring for the bag will be woven in toward the end of the project.

Step 12: Continue tying rows of single alternating square knots.

Step 13: Stop tying alternating square knots once there are 17 rows total.

Step 14: Pick any spot at the bottom to tie one additional alternating square knot. This is where the bottom seam will start.

Step 15: Push that entire square knot back inside the bag, also pushing all of its loose strings inside as well so that those strings will not get tangled in the next knots.

Step 16: Grab the next two strings on each side of that first knot, joining them together for the next square knot.

Step 17: Tie a square knot as tightly as possible with those four strings, then push this square knot and its loose strings inside the bag.

Step 18: Continue to tie new square knots to close the "seam," moving on to the next two strings on each side of the previous knots.

Step 19: Repeat the process until all strings are tied and all loose strings are on the inside of the bag.

Step 20: Flip the bag inside out. Trim all the loose strings to just about 1 inch (2.5 cm) long.

Step 21: Turn the bag right side out again. Cut the accent color string to 30 inches (76.2 cm) in length and weave the string in and out of the row of double square knots to form a drawstring.

Step 22: Add a bead to each side and tie a knot underneath each bead to secure in place.

Step 23: Cinch the bag closed by pulling the drawstring.

Step 24: Cut one piece of main color string to 5 feet (1.5 m) in length and another to 30 feet (9.1 m) in length. Attach the 5-foot (1.5-m) length of string to the center of the clasp using a lark's head knot.

Step 25: Attach the 30-foot (9.1-m) length of string to the keychain around the first string using a lark's head knot, so that the two longer strings are on the outside.

Step 26: Tie a square knot approximately 1 inch (2.5 cm) below the clasp.

Step 27: Tie continuous square knots until the square knot chain reaches approximately 42 inches (106.7 cm) in length.

Step 28: Feed the end strings through the other keychain clasp.

Step 29: Fold the strings over the clasp with about 1 inch (2.5 cm) of space between the last knot and the clasp.

Step 30: Cut two more strings into 30-inch (76.2-cm) lengths, then tie gathering knots directly under each keychain clasp to cover the space between the clasp and the first knot.

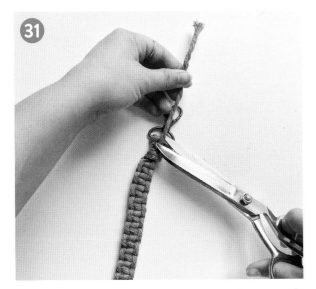

Step 31: Trim off the excess cords on the top and bottom of the gathering knots.

Step 32: Attach the keychain clasps to opposite sides of the top of the bag.

FEATHER WALL HANGING

level: intermediate/advanced

This wall hanging is more of a classic layered style, but with a feathery twist. Beaded accents and fluffy fringe take this simple and modern piece to the next level, adding a boho element that is subtle enough to fit into a variety of home décor styles. This wall hanging expands upon the feather technique used in the Macramé Feather (page 151), but uses the feathers as accents in a larger piece. Becoming more familiar with clove hitch knots and layered techniques will help set you up for success in making this intermediate- to advanced-level wall hanging.

materials

- 5mm white string: 672 feet (204.8 m)
- 30-inch (76.2-cm) branch or dowel
- Measuring tape
- Scissors
- 16 to 18 wide-mouth beads
- Comb
- Optional: S-hooks and working rack

knots used in this project

- Reverse Lark's Head Knot (page 10)
- Diagonal Clove Hitch Knot (page 15)
- Square Knot (page 13)
- Single Strand Lark's Head Knot (page 11)
- Alternating Colors Square Knot Method (page 21)
- Lark's Head Knot (page 10)

layer 1

Step 1: Cut eight strings into 12-foot (3.7-m) lengths. Divide the strings into two groups of four strings, then attach each group to the branch about 11 inches (27.9 cm) in from either end of the branch using a reverse lark's head knot. Pick a side to start on.

Step 2: Pick up the fourth string (counting from the outside in) and cross it diagonally inward over the rest of the strings. This will be the first lead cord.

Step 3: Tie a row of four diagonal clove hitch knots.

Step 4: Pick up the fourth string in again, this time crossing it diagonally outward over the rest of the strings (in the opposite direction from the first row).

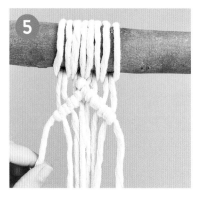

Step 5: Tie a row of three diagonal clove hitch knots. This should create an inverted "V" shape for the top half of the diamond pattern.

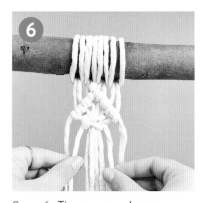

Step 6: Tie a square knot using the two outer cords within the diamond.

Step 7: Use the same lead cords to tie two rows of diagonal clove hitch knots into a "V" shape to complete the bottom half of the diamond.

Step 8: Continue tying four diamond patterns on both groups of strings on the branch.

Step 9: Join the two sections in the center using the four center strings.

Step 10: Tie one more diamond pattern using the four center strings from each section.

Step 11: Cut 24 pieces of string into 65-inch (165.1-cm) lengths. Attach three strings at a time to each outer string of the diamond pattern using a reverse lark's head knot.

layer 2

Step 12: Cut eight more strings into 15-foot (4.6-m) lengths. Separate them into two groups of four strings. Use a reverse lark's head knot to attach each group of four strings to the branch approximately 2 inches (5 cm) out from the last section.

Step 13: Using the same diamond pattern in steps 2 to 7, create seven diamonds on each side.

Step 14: Join the two sections in the center using the four center strings from each side to tie one more diamond.

layer 3

Step 15: Cut eight more strings into 12-foot (3.7-m) lengths. Divide them into two groups of four strings each, then use a reverse lark's head knot to attach each group of four strings to the branch approximately 4 inches (10 cm) out from the last section.

Step 16: Tie five diamond patterns down each side, using the same instructions from steps 2 to 7 in layer 1.

Step 17: Direct the outer layer toward the midpoint of layer 2, matching the end of the outer layer directly underneath the fourth diamond in the middle layer.

Step 18: Use the inner string to tie a single strand lark's head knot to the outer string directly under the fourth diamond, securing both sections together.

Step 19: For extra stability, attach another string from that section directly underneath the first attachment using a single strand lark's head knot. (I chose to use a string that was three strings below the first.)

Step 20: Repeat steps 16 to 19 on the other side.

Step 21: Cut 46 strings into 45-inch (114.3-cm) lengths. Attach 15 groups of three strings to the outer strings of the last layer of diamonds using a reverse lark's head knot. Then, attach the last string to the middle layer of diamonds, beneath where the outer layer is connected.

Step 22: Find the two center strings from the lowest diamond, and then slide a wide-mouth bead up the strings to the top.

Step 23: Cut 30 strings into 15-inch (38.1-cm) lengths. Divide them into five groups of six strings; each group will be used to create a feather. Starting with where the bead was just attached in the center, use the alternating colors square knot method to attach six strings directly under the bead.

Step 24: Once all strings are attached, trim them into a rough feather shape.

Step 25: Use a comb to brush out all of the fringe.

Step 26: Do a final trim of the feather, making sure all the ends are cut smoothly and evenly.

Step 27: Count up one diamond on each side, and attach another feather (with or without adding a bead first; I chose to leave this one without) to a pair of strings above that diamond. Then, count up another one or two diamonds on each side, and attach another feather (I added a bead this time) to another pair of strings.

Step 28: Repeat step 27 on the other side of the wall hanging. Comb and trim each feather until all five are completed.

Step 29: Cut 10 pieces of string into 12-inch (30.5-cm) lengths. Use a lark's head knot to attach them to the strings just above where all the fringe was attached on the outer layer.

Step 30: Use the comb to brush the added strings into tassels, then trim them to approximately 3-inch (7.6-cm) lengths.

Step 31: Thread a 10-inch (25.4-cm) continuous length of beads onto a 10-foot (3-m) piece of string, with the beads in the center. Use a single strand lark's head knot on both ends of the beads to secure it to the branch in the center, just between the first layers.

Step 32: Give the piece a final trim, cutting a "V" shape to the desired length.

ACKNOWLEDGMENTS

First and foremost, I would like to thank my partner, Joshua James Alvarez, for being my main source of support throughout the creation of this book. I could not have done this without you being there for me, picking up the slack when I had deadlines to reach, encouraging me every step of the way even when I doubted myself, and reassuring me that I would create something that many people would love.

To my sister Lauren, my mom Becky, and my dad Ron, thank you for encouraging me and being there whenever I needed help, advice, or encouragement in my journey as an artist in general as well as in this new journey of sharing my art with others.

To Sophia Acosta, my talented friend and photographer for all of the nature scenes in this book, thank you for taking my vision and bringing it to life in a way that was more beautiful than I could have imagined.

To my friends Victoria, Nick, and Luis, who always believed in me and told me in the beginning of my macramé journey that I was going places even when I didn't see it yet.

To Kristen and Noelle, for constantly pushing and inspiring me to grow in my art and as a human, and for being my community and support through all of it.

To my incredible editors Emily, Sarah, and the talented publishing team at Page Street, thank you for guiding me every step of the way in bringing these ideas to life, and helping me to share my passion with the world. I truly couldn't have done this without you as my guides! And a huge thank you to Emma Hardy and the entire design team for making this book a visual masterpiece in itself. This has been an unforgettable experience and I am so thankful for every single person that helped bring this book from beyond my wildest dreams into reality!

And last but not least, thank you to my fiber art community. The friends I have made in this community mean so much to me, and they have uplifted me time and time again.

ABOUT THE AUTHOR

Rachel Breuklander is a fiber artist based in Los Angeles, California. She began learning macramé in 2016 as a creative outlet and quickly developed a passion for the craft. Now, this is her full-time creative pursuit. When she isn't tangled in a mess of string, she loves to spend time in nature hiking with her pup Finn, camping in the mountains, or searching for driftwood. Her love of spending time in nature fuels her work, and eventually her passion for nature inspired her to create the unique macramé "landscapes" that she is now well known for.

Now, she shares her love for this art form with others by creating larger scale, one-of-a-kind pieces and by teaching classes and workshops, as well as by providing online education and support to other budding macramé artists and enthusiasts. She firmly believes that everyone has a creative side, and macramé is a fantastic way to explore and develop that creativity. She also encourages other makers' exploration into the world of fiber crafts by supplying eco-friendly macramé materials, DIY kits, and other fiber supplies.

INDEX